07601750

CHANDOS
INFORMATION PROFESSIONAL SERIES

Series Editor: Ruth Rikowski
(email: Rikowskigr@aol.com)

Chandos' new series of books are aimed at the busy information professional. They have been specially commissioned to provide the reader with an authoritative view of current thinking. They are designed to provide easy-to-read and (most importantly) practical coverage of topics that are of interest to librarians and other information professionals. If you would like a full listing of current and forthcoming titles, please visit our web site **www.chandospublishing.com** or contact Hannah Grace-Williams on email info@chandospublishing.com or telephone number +44 (0) 1993 848726.

New authors: we are always pleased to receive ideas for new titles; if you would like to write a book for Chandos, please contact Dr Glyn Jones on email gjones@chandospublishing.com or telephone number +44 (0) 1993 848726.

Bulk orders: some organisations buy a number of copies of our books. If you are interested in doing this, we would be pleased to discuss a discount. Please contact Hannah Grace-Williams on email info@chandospublishing.com or telephone number +44 (0) 1993 848726.

Marketing the Best Deal in Town: Your Library

Where is your Purple Owl?

NANCY ROSSITER

Chandos Publishing
Oxford · England

Chandos Publishing (Oxford) Limited
TBAC Business Centre
Avenue 4
Station Lane
Witney
Oxford OX28 4BN
UK
Tel: +44 (0) 1993 848726 Fax: +44 (0) 1865 884448
Email: info@chandospublishing.com
www.chandospublishing.com

First published in Great Britain in 2008

ISBN:
978 1 84334 305 9 (paperback)
978 1 84334 306 6 (hardback)
1 84334 305 3 (paperback)
1 84334 306 1 (hardback)

British Library Cataloguing-in-Publication Data.
A catalogue record for this book is available from the British Library.

Typeset by Avocet Typeset, Chilton, Aylesbury, Bucks.
Printed in the UK and USA.

Contents

Contents

Acknowledgements

There are a number of people who were instrumental in getting this book off the ground. Many of these people were my students at the Graduate School of Library and Information Science (GSLIS), Simmons College in Boston, Massachusetts. The discussions in my LIS 477 Marketing the Library Class – particularly during the Spring semester 2007 – were some of the best ever at Simmons. The students were passionate about their libraries and brought up both challenging issues as well as very creative solutions. In particular, I'd like to thank Sarah Belanich, Sarah Bordac (Brown University Library), Sarah Feldman, Keri Hammond, Kelly Linehan, Matthew Mitchell (Trinity College Library), Larisa Shvarts, Stephanie Temple, Abigail Thompson, Catherine Mulencamp, and Susan Sinnott. Their work and several of their ideas have been incorporated in various chapters throughout the text. Other contributing students include Ann Rust, Michelle Angel, Marie McAndrew-Taylor, and Karen Weis.

Additionally, Debbie Hoadly, Assistant Director from the Plaistow Public Library in Plaistow, New Hampshire, as well as a former student, helped immensely with her ideas, pictures and hard work. She amazed me and the other students in class with her well thought out marketing initiatives.

I'd also like to thank the Bryant University Library and

Portsmouth Public Library for providing friendly, helpful customer service to me while writing this text. Linda Watkins, Simmons College's GISLIS librarian, as always, was also a great resource.

And, although I know that they will never read this, I'd like to thank Tom Peters, Seth Godin, and Faith Popcorn. It would be a real kick to meet them someday.

Thanks again everyone for your help!!

Introduction

As an Assistant Professor at Simmons College's Graduate School of Library and Information Science (GSLIS), I have always had a challenge in choosing texts for my classes. I generally found that books written for business classes had a lot of material (and a high price tag) that was not specific enough for libraries. Examples used to illustrate concepts throughout these texts were usually about large corporations that students found difficult to relate library experiences to. On the other hand, there were various library texts that appeared to be missing something. For many semesters in my 'Marketing the Library' classes, I tried to combine one of Kotler's short marketing texts with various library marketing texts. The students, perhaps due to the comparison with Kotler, found many of the library texts dull and uninspiring. During my continual search for a text that would work, Chandos Publishing contacted me about writing a book. I knew I had to take a shot a writing a marketing text that could be used by academics as well as practitioners, that was written in a straightforward way, incorporating cases and exercises, as well as borrowing ideas from the top minds in the business world (egads!) and applying them to libraries. So here goes.

The language, style, and tone of this book are very different from my first book *Making a Difference: Leadership and Academic Libraries*, written with Peter

Hernon. Nowhere in that text will you find references to peeing on ideas (p. 74, doggie mouthwash (p. 54), retching (p. 88), or dog-vertising (p. 94). The thought behind the writing of this text was designed to match the energy and excitement of the topic of marketing. I hope you will be inspired to create a marketing plan or new innovations to make your library remarkable.

A quick note about the subtitle: much of the inspiration for this text comes form Seth Godin's 'Purple Cow.' Many libraries use an owl as their mascot, hence the 'Purple Owl.' Here's to hoping you find one in your library.

About the author

Nancy Rossiter has been a professor, writer, entrepreneur, author, and mentor for the past ten years. As an Assistant Professor at Simmons College's Graduate School of Library and Information Science, Nancy taught Marketing the Library, Information Entrepreneurship, and Management classes and was a much sought-after speaker on library issues. Her first book *Making a Difference: Leadership in Academic Libraries* with Peter Hernon was published in 2007. She has also taught at Bryant University, Providence College, and Worcester Polytechnic Institute, and is currently an Assistant Professor at the Davis College of Business at Jacksonville University. She has an MBA from Bryant University and a doctorate from the University of Sarasota. Nancy enjoys reading, gardening, rehabbing old homes, and jogging, and has been a competitive triathlete. She lives in Amelia Island, Florida with her rescued collies, Holly and Elsie.

The author may contacted via the publishers or at:

thebigwho@juno.com

Why market libraries?

Introduction

Chances are pretty good your library does not have a formal marketing plan. When several libraries were contacted for the purpose of writing this book, most librarians (and directors) stated that their library does not 'do' marketing, in spite of having a website, several flyers promoting upcoming programs, and other various marketing activities that apparently were not recognized as being 'marketing.' This chapter will discuss these reasons and present solutions for overcoming common obstacles for library marketing.

Problems

Did you see that great Super Bowl ad for your local library during the big game? No? Why not? Of course, the thought of libraries advertising on the Super Bowl may seem ridiculous. Why? Here are a few:

- money (lack thereof);
- attitude towards marketing;
- complexity of marketing in libraries; and

- lack of knowledge of what marketing is (confusion of marketing with advertising, for example).

Money

In 2007, advertisers paid approximately 2.6 million dollars for a 30-second spot during Super Bowl XLI[1] … That's a lot of late fees. Lack of money to spend on advertising is often cited as one of the main barriers to library marketing. However, marketing library services is not just a matter of spending money (and in the case of the Super Bowl truckloads of it!). Marketing also includes improving patron's experiences with library services. The way that the director and staff interact with library customers is what shapes their experiences and 'markets' the library to these customers. Advertising will be discussed in greater depth in Chapter 2.

Attitude

A closely related issue is the attitude of librarians towards marketing. In the past, for many information professionals 'marketing was regarded as an alien commercial process, inconsistent with the values of customer service.' [2] Many librarians feel that the value of library services should be apparent to all, and therefore marketing is unnecessary. 'Hucksterish' connotations are also associated with marketing – something borrowed from the 'for profit' sector that has no place in the library world.

Complexity

Additionally, the marketing of libraries is a complex task. Libraries offer a wide range of services (books, DVDs,

Internet access) to a diverse group of users (seniors, children, faculty, and students). To complicate this issue, many librarians do not have the training in or the knowledge of marketing tools and techniques. Few library schools offer marketing as part of their curriculum or include discussion of marketing in required or core classes.[3] So why bother to market information services?

Case Study 1.1

Brookline Public Library

The Brookline Public Library is the third busiest library in Massachusetts. The library is greatly supported by its community, and has always been at the 'center of the social and cultural life of Brookline.'[4] Its current director has been in the position since 1992.

A small amount of promotion is done to advertise the library's programs and services. For the most part, this promotion is for specific programs being offered at the library, and not promotion for its core services. It is the director's belief that the community already strongly supports the library's core services, and any further promotion of them would not be an effective use of resources. According to the director, the only outcome from this type of promotion would be to attract too many users to the library – circulation is already extremely high, and if anyone else was coming to the library, the library would not have enough resources to support the increase in use.[5]

Reasons for marketing library services

First and most importantly, libraries face either a decreasing resource base or stronger competition for existing resources.

The current resources are further constrained by the need to increase the range of services. As a result, convenience of these services usually declines, most often in the form of shorter service hours, fewer staff, and a drop in locally owned information resources.[6] Public libraries have to compete for public funding that provides for its existence. Funding for special libraries is frequently targeted during the parent organization's budget cuts. Library marketing benefits the bottom line of the organization.[7]

In addition to competing for funding, libraries are also competing for customers. Libraries are part of the competitive service industry which faces competition from online book dealers such as Amazon.com, mega bookstores such as Barnes & Noble and Borders, consultants, Google, and many others. In a recent article, Cynthia Shamel found that the user is the biggest competitor for library services. We are taught at a young age to go to the library, not use the librarian. This leads to the popular thought that people can get the same results as they could get from a librarian by 'Googling' it themselves.[8]

Philip Kotler gets to the heart of why all nonprofits need to market themselves in his book *Strategic Marketing for Nonprofit Organizations*. He argues:

> Today nonprofit organizations are operating under more changes and pressures than ever before. Without closely monitored and implemented marketing strategies designed to take the organization through a particular course of action, and without the ability to change course should the need arise, an organization risks being lost in the throes of internal economic upheaval.[9]

Pretty serious stuff.

Navigating the obstacles

In general, any change in any organization must be supported by the people at the top. Connecting marketing with the library's mission is a critical step. It is imperative to ensure that the upper levels of the library (trustees, deans, presidents, directors) are aware of why the library needs to be marketed and buy into a marketing program.

Overcoming the funding obstacle will be discussed in Chapter 6. There are many low-cost solutions to finding marketing dollars, and if the top management in the library truly believes in the value of marketing, money will be found.

The three related problems of attitude, complexity, and lack of knowledge can be tackled early on by integrating marketing courses into the library school curriculum. For librarians, staff and administration without an MLS (Masters in Library Science) or even those currently holding an MLS, continuing professional development may be the key to realizing the value of marketing the library.

In 'Marketing the worth of your library,'[10] Rivka K. Sass discusses five ways libraries can market their worth. She suggests having a 'real' budget for advertising rather than depending on donated advertising. She also suggests that when using public service announcements, they should be targeted at Gen X and Gen Y audiences, as they are the ones most likely to be watching late at night when these spots are most likely to be shown. Sass's third suggestion is to use the outside of buses to advertise the value of the staff at the library. Another idea is to use a rolling reference cart so that you can be where the people are. The Brown University Library in Providence, Rhode Island is currently using this idea. Sass's final suggestion is to create product-specific marketing materials through working with database vendors to get the word out about the e-resources the library offers.

The cases that follow allow you to apply the ideas from the chapter to real-life library situations. Have fun!

Case study 1.2

Problems in Plainville

The Plainville Public Library is located in Central Connecticut, 14 miles southwest of Hartford. The town of Plainville measures 9.6 square miles and boasts a population density of 1,742 people per square mile. According to the Plainville Public Library's Long-Range Plan, the mission of the library is to 'provide excellent service to meet the educational, informational, and cultural needs of Plainville's citizens through its collections and programs.' The Plainville Public Library Director reports to a six-member, elected Board of Trustees. The library staff includes three professional librarians, four full-time paraprofessionals, and nine part-time clerks and pages. Under the director, staff members are divided into three functional units: Children's Services, Adult and Technical Services, and Circulation.

The pervading stereotype of a public library is that of an outdated institution reluctant to adapt to the latest technology and unwilling to promote its services to the public. While perceptions may be derived from elements of truth, examination of the Plainville Public Library and its marketing strategy reveals that at least one public library in many ways defies this stereotype. Plainville Library has identified the strengths and weaknesses of its collection and identified a marketing strategy that complements these qualities and works within the parameters of a public institution constrained by staff and budget limitations. While there is still significant room for growth in terms of marketing initiatives, the librarians have already seized a number of opportunities to promote their institution in a tasteful and effective fashion.

Problems
As far as the major difficulties associated with developing and implementing marketing plans for the Plainville Public Library are

6

concerned, six primary challenges were identified. The first challenge involves changing demographics within Plainville and surrounding towns, namely a marked increase in Spanish and Polish-speaking residents. The staff became aware of such individuals because they walked into the library and requested materials in Spanish and Polish. Currently, the three librarians at Plainville Library are pondering how these persons – who definitely seem interested in using the library – can best be targeted. The second challenge is that the library has no specific funding for marketing initiatives – each of the individual components comprising any marketing program is charged separately (for instance, staff time comes out of payroll, flyers come out of materials, etc.). The only exception to this rule is made for the children's summer reading program, which is funded by the Friends of the Library, a group of individuals who offer membership dues and services in support of the Plainville Library.

The remaining challenges are intertwined in that they all relate to the process of adapting an institution that for many years served a largely unchallenged public service role to a new environment with many competing entities. The first of these challenges (and the third overall challenge) is the lack of staff at the Plainville Library trained in marketing techniques. As library schools have not traditionally offered marketing courses, it is imperative that librarians and their staff develop such skills on the job. The fourth challenge is the reluctance of some paraprofessional staff members to participate in marketing activities. The reluctance of such staff members to market the library stems primarily from a perception of themselves as already having too many tasks to perform each day. The fifth challenge is staff resistance to change, which is derived from an admirable commitment, yet sometimes limiting attachment, to the provision of traditional library services. The sixth and final challenge to marketing the Plainville Public Library is the public's perception that libraries are boring places with only books and that the Internet makes such facilities obsolete.

Of course, within challenges opportunities can be found, and at the Plainville Library two of the aforementioned challenges in particular have prompted much thought in terms of marketing possibilities. Regarding the sixth challenge of changing the public's perception of the library, it is certain that if people knew of the materials and services available through the library in addition to books – books on CD, music CDs, DVDs, free Internet access, and access to research databases – they would be far more inclined to frequent and make use of the library. The music CDs and DVDs purchased by the library are, for the most part, new releases – in general, the library receives a newly released DVD at the same time as Blockbuster. While the librarians have not yet devised a concrete strategy for publicizing these offerings, they recognize the importance of doing so and are currently contemplating various avenues for achieving this goal. In terms of the second challenge of attracting Spanish- and Polish-speaking residents to the library, such individuals are prime candidates for library patronage – they may need assistance with learning English or with job searches, endeavors that can be greatly facilitated by library resources. Plans for targeting these potential patrons include the drafting of a press release to be disseminated to local newspapers as well as the creation of signage to identify the location of relevant materials in the library. (Of course, it still remains to be seen how these materials will be translated into the proper languages without Spanish- or Polish-speaking individuals on the library staff!)

In evaluating these marketing-related challenges and related areas of opportunity, there are a few areas of overarching concern which are worth mentioning. First, they wonder if, in the process of identifying demographic groups to target – such as foreign-language speakers – they have overlooked populations that might potentially be more loyal, frequent, and high-profile library users. For instance, currently, the Plainville Library does not hold the patronage of many teenagers. The children's librarian does not purchase many young adult titles or devote her time to courting the young adult demographic because it is considered too difficult to keep up with their ever-changing tastes. However, if the library could actually launch a successful marketing campaign aimed at teenagers, it would bring a large and influential population into the building and ultimately garner much recognition for the institution.

While the first area of concern is related to strategic planning, the second two areas have to do with the mission and nature of a public library. As a non-profit institution that operates based upon a budget and is first and foremost responsible for providing the public with information services, the Plainville Library faces inherent constraints in terms of its marketing possibilities. To begin with, the library cannot focus so much on marketing activities that critical library functions are neglected (all paraprofessional staff can work only a prescribed number of hours per week). Secondly, the question always arises of how a marketing campaign can be funded. As was mentioned earlier, there is no separate marketing budget; if such a budget existed, surely Plainville Library would already have implemented a number of more ambitious marketing initiatives. Occasionally the Friends of the Library will support a project, but, in general, they cannot make multiple, major contributions. A number of grants are available that will pay for specific programs, including the marketing of a program.

Looking towards the future, as the world changes, marketing challenges for the Plainville Library will, in many ways, stay the same. Demographics will continue to shift, prompting the library to target these new populations, and technology will continue to rapidly advance, forcing the library to promote its technology-based services.

Case Study 1.3

Dighton Public Library

The Dighton Public Library (DPL) is located in a small rural community in southeastern Massachusetts. The library serves mostly residents of Dighton and some residents of neighboring communities. About half of the current users are under the age of 15; the next largest group is women over 60. The group that uses the library services least often is childless adults between 35 and 50, particularly men. Many young families use the library together when the children are young but less often or not at all as the children reach high-school age. Most visitors to the library must drive; there is no parking lot, limited on-street parking and no public transportation. The library also serves virtual users who never enter the building but use the services available online.

The current staff consists of four part-time employees: the director, circulation, catalogue, and children's librarians. The library is open six days and 40 hours per week; it is publicly funded with local taxes.

There is no direct funding for marketing. All internal marketing is done as part of the daily operations and staff training. Indirect funding of the marketing plan is through one of the three supportive library organizations or through the Friends of the Library group. The Friends of the Library pay for the printing and mailing of a quarterly newsletter, which is prepared by a professional graphic artist pro bono. These newsletters include promotions of library programs and public relations articles about the library services.

Unpaid advertisement is done through the local cable station, school weekly newsletters, and program announcements in local newspapers. Flyers are distributed throughout the town at businesses, post offices, town buildings, and schools.

The biggest challenge is the inadequate space to offer all the programs and services that are requested by the customers and to house the collection. This also causes problems with the need to limit attendees at programs and turn away customers. The small size of the building also prevents usage and certain population groups feel uncomfortable in such a crowded space with no quiet study or reference space. Funding is always a concern but the community continues to increase the annual budget requests. The next major funding concern is to fund a new building so the town can make full use of all the services the library could potentially offer.

DPL's marketing plan

Even a small rural public library with a very limited budget and no marketing professional on staff can develop and manage a marketing plan. Administration must recognize that staff are the library's internal customers, users are external customers, and other stakeholders include selectmen, finance committee members, trustees and other elected officials. Well trained staff that know and agree with the library's vision can have a significant impact on the success of the library's marketing plan. If you find yourself in a similar situation as DPL, the chapters that follow will help to get you thinking about your marketing plan and what you need to do in order to market your library more effectively.

Exercise 1.1   Dighton Library marketing

What should the library do to market itself better to the community?

Exercise 1.2   Overcoming marketing barriers in your library

What unique challenges to creating a marketing program does your library face? Why do you need to market your library? Are there any services or programs your library offers that could benefit from marketing? How can these challenges be overcome?

Suggestions for further reading

Kotler, Philip (1999) *Kotler on Marketing*. New York: Free Press.
Kotler, Philip (2006) *Strategic Marketing for Nonprofit Organizations*, 6th edn. Ventura, CA: Academic Internet Publishers.
Weingand, Darlene (1999) *Marketing/Planning Library and Information Services*, 2nd edn. Westport, CT: Libraries Unlimited.

Notes

1. Paul La Monica, 'Super prices for Super Bowl ads,' available at: *http://money.cnn.com/2007/01/03/news/funny/superbowl_ads/index.htm* (accessed 17 July 2007).

2. Jennifer Rowley (2003) 'Information marketing: seven questions,' *Library Management*, 24 (1): 13–19.

3. See 'TEN reasons for marketing library and information services,' available at: *http://clips.lis.uiuc.edu/2003_09 .html#03* (accessed 17 July 2007).

4. The Public Library of Brookline. See: *http://www .brooklinelibrary.org* (accessed 24 April 2007).

5. Chuck Flaherty (2007) Personal Interview. Brookline, MA.

6. G. Edward Evans, Patricia Layzell Ward, and Bendik Rugaas (2007) *Management Basics for Information Professionals*. New York: Neal Schuman.

7. Cynthia Shamel, 'Building a brand: got librarian?' available at: *http://www.infotoday.com/searcher/jul02/shamel.htm* (accessed 17 July 2007).

9. Philip Kotler (2002) *Strategic Marketing for Nonprofit Organizations*. Englewood Cliffs, NJ: Prentice Hall.

10. Rivka K. Sass (2002) 'Marketing the worth of your library,' *Library Journal*, 15 June.

2

The language of marketing

Introduction

This chapter will discuss basic marketing terminology. So if you've had a marketing class or are already familiar with marketing terms, skip this chapter and see if the rest of the book makes sense. If this is your first venture into the field of marketing, this chapter is for you.

What is marketing?

In his book *Strategic Marketing for Nonprofit Organizations*, Philip Kotler defines nonprofit marketing as:

> the function of a nonprofit whose goal is to plan, price, promote, and distribute the organization's programs and products by keeping in constant touch with the organization's various constituencies, uncovering their needs and expectations for the organization and themselves, and building a program of communication to not only express the organization's purpose and goals, but also their mutually beneficial want-satisfying products.[1]

What a sentence! Kotler has combined the 4 Ps (discussed next) and thrown in the importance of market research (Chapter 7) along with designing products and services that fill the needs (wants) of their constituencies (Chapter 4). The takeaway here is that marketing involves several interrelated functions and by doing these functions correctly, we can better serve our constituencies. Kotler also includes '[marketing] requires innovation and a willingness to change'[2] which are critical elements in this book. As the adage goes, 'If you don't like change, you're going to like irrelevance even less.'[3] If you are unwilling to innovate or change, you are wasting your time reading this text!

The 4 Ps of marketing

You are bound to find at least four 'Ps' that describe the components of marketing in any marketing textbook you pick up. The traditional four Ps consist of product, place, price, and promotion. Several textbook authors also include positioning as a separate P. Seth Godin includes a 'Purple Cow' in his list of Ps (Purple Cows will be discussed in Chapter 5). Here we will discuss the 4 Ps as they relate to marketing libraries.

Product

The library's 'products' are the programs and services the library offers to its customers. These products include interlibrary loan, references services, children's programming, web access and many others. Many marketing texts suggest differentiating your products, features, and benefits – a feature is something that is intrinsic to the product and benefits consist of the intangible reward experienced though the product. For example, the books and reference services (feature) provide resources for lifetime learning (benefit). The library building (feature) provides space for the community to gather and learn (benefit). Marketers tend focus on the benefits in promoting organizations, as this tends to be more effective than just listing features and hoping the customer will provide the associated benefits.

Place

OK, you got me. The second P is actually a D – it really should be 'distribution' instead of place. But isn't it easier to remember four Ps than three Ps and one D? So the word 'place' was substituted for distribution to keep it simple, but it does tend to confuse people that focus on the narrow meaning of the word. Essentially, place refers to how customers and products are connected; in traditional business terms it means the channel of distribution from the manufacturer to the customer. In library terms, it is basically how a product gets to the library and from the library to the customer. These distribution channels can include online catalogs, databases, electronic connections, and interlibrary delivery services, as well as the traditional understanding of the library as a physical place where patrons come to get the library's products. The library as a physical place attracts and retains customers. The layout of the library, appropriate signage, comfortable furniture, Internet access throughout the library, availability of copy machines and printers, attentive and helpful personnel – all contribute to attracting customers and making them to want to return.

Price

A price is typically an amount charged for a product or service. Traditionally the library's services are free except, for example, for overdue fines, copying, printing, movie rentals, and some research services. However, every service and product has its price. Books and other materials cost money, personnel require salary, furniture, office equipment and supplies, computers – everything has a price, plus other direct and indirect expenses occur. Consider also what a trip to the library is worth to users in terms of time to get to the library, time to learn the systems, or time to use the services. The state of Maine has created a value use calculator that enables users to calculate how much their library is worth to them. Items include the number of books, magazines, videos, and audio books borrowed, hours of computer use, interlibrary loan, etc., so that patrons can see how much the library saves them in real dollars.[4]

Promotion

Libraries operate in a competitive environment and must be creative with services and products they deliver to the customers. It means that they must advertise their services and make themselves distinguishable and recognizable as information providers. Some libraries advertise through the website and via e-mails, as well as through printed materials such as flyers, brochures, magnets, and cards. Others offer incentives when promoting programs and special events. These incentives include coupons to local restaurants, gifts, and museum passes. Some libraries also create awareness among the community, so-called 'buzz' about the library (discussed in Chapter 9), so that more people know what it has to offer. The following case illustrates the marketing mix at work in an academic library.

Trinity College Library's marketing mix

The Raether Library and Information Technology Center at Trinity College (hereafter referred to as Trinity College Library or the Library) comprises the library facilities of Trinity College, a small liberal arts undergraduate college in Hartford, Connecticut. The Trinity College Library includes the Watkinson Library which contains the Trinity College archives and rare books collection.

The 'products' or rather services that Trinity College and Watkinson Libraries provide are twofold: first and foremost they provide access to information for their patrons; second, they provide a place for events such as lectures and exhibitions. While these two services are important, the task in marketing is to differentiate them from the same services provided by other libraries in the greater Hartford area. One of the ways to do this is to market the uniqueness of the resources and information that the Watkinson can provide to the greater public. The library and the College both lament the fact that it is an information repository often under-utilized both by students and the greater public. The collections in the Watkinson mostly include rare primary sources that are not easily accessible in other locations, including historical documents and treatises, early imprints of many works of English and American literature, ornithological works of many different eras, etc. While exhibitions are used to highlight parts of the collection, these often attract only those outside the College who are interested in books rather than students and faculty members from within the College. The ideal use of the product in the marketing mix would attract both target markets to the Library, not only to see the exhibits, but also to use the vast array of other resources in the Watkinson.

For the main Library, the product that is highlighted in the marketing mix is often not the books and information the Library can provide. Instead, the service that is marketed is a place to sit and study.

Emphasis is placed on the comforts that the Library can provide for studying, including comfortable furniture, the café, and beautiful surroundings. In addition, the technological aspects of the building are also highlighted, including the large number of places to plug in a laptop (which extends, interestingly, to the garden area in front of the building) and the number of computer stations in the building. In essence, the service and the distribution center (i.e. the two Ps product and place in the marketing mix) are conflated in this case.

However, place is also important on its own. In an era when libraries are often looking at ways to downsize due to the proliferation of digital resources that do not take up the same amount of space as books, Trinity College mounted an extensive renovation and addition to its library between 2000 and 2003, signaling a commitment to the Library as the center of the campus. It also marked a shift in the image the Library projected. First, the renovation caused a name change from Trinity College Library to Raether Library and Information Technology Center. This was primarily the result of moving the Computing Center into the new building to demonstrate the link between the missions of the two institutions. In this way, the Library could market itself as a technologically advanced institution that distributed information by both traditional and new means. As stated above, the Library as a place has become a product of the Library in its own right. Much of the space in the new addition is not stack space, but study areas, including the introduction of group study rooms and a stunning two-floor reading room. Increasingly, among faculty and students alike, the Library has become a place to go and interact on a more comfortable level. The Library uses place as a marketing tool mainly through its location on campus. It is in a central location, easily accessible from both faculty offices and student dormitories. However, it is not actively marketed except through marketing for lectures or exhibits, or through tours that all first-year students take as part of their first-year seminar.

In the digital age, a second 'place' is asserting itself: the Library web location. With the proliferation of digital materials, distribution of inform-ation can occur just about anywhere that a reliable Internet connection can be found. The website of the Library is accessible from the main Trinity web page; however, the Library's main page includes both the Library and the computing center, requiring another mouse-click to get to the actual Library webpage. Nevertheless, the digital place that the Library occupies is fairly easy to navigate, including links to both the catalog and, more importantly, the Trinity Online Resources page to access digital materials. By placing the link in a prominent place on the website with a description of what information it contains, the Library is marketing it as a place of distribution. The digital place is used in marketing through bibliographic instruction workshops that are taught to all first-year students and reinforced for upperclassmen in research-intensive courses.

Price is not often used as a marketing tool in marketing the Trinity College Library. All services of the Library are free to students and faculty, including lectures and exhibitions. This is used primarily as a tool to draw people from outside the College who might not otherwise attend an event on campus. The College Library usually stays away from using price as a marketing tool within the College community, except for a line at the end of an announcement that states the event is free, because students are acutely aware of the price of the Trinity education. Because Library events are looked upon as an extension of the Trinity education, they are free for students and faculty.

Promotion of the Library is done via announcements through mass e-mailings and postings on Trinity Exchange, a website that lists all of the events happening at the College and that sends out a digest-style e-mail once or twice a day with all of the recent postings to all members of the College community. In addition, posters are placed around campus announcing the event, an article appears in the *Trinity Tripod*, the main newspaper for the College, and fliers are often placed in student mailboxes. By using both digital and non-digital means, the Library attempts to capture the widest segment of the College community. For promotion outside of the College, the *Hartford Courant* is often used as the vehicle of choice for promotion, in addition to the website of the College and the Library. A mailing list is also maintained by the Library so that mailings sent to students and faculty about events can also be sent to those in the greater community who have expressed a genuine interest in the Library.

Exercise 2.1   Creating a marketing mix

Outline a market mix for each of the following:

- *a radically new design for a toothbrush;*
- *a new breakthrough drug;*
- *a new library program: 'Reading to Infants.'*

The promotional mix

The promotional mix consists of advertising, personal selling, public relations, and sales promotions. The goal behind promotion is usually summed up in the acronym AIDA. The first 'A' stands for Attention. Gaining your customer's attention is the first step in your promotional campaign. It's what separates your message from the rest of the pack. The 'I' stands for Interest. Once you have the customer's attention, you want to generate their interest in your services. The 'D' stands for desire. Once you've generated attention and interest, you want them to desire your services. This is often done by creating an appeal to your patrons' emotions. Finally, the last 'A' stands for Action. You want your promotional efforts to generate action in your customers, for example to come to the library to experience your programs. The following sections will discuss the various elements of the promotional mix.

Advertising

Advertising is a paid form of communication between the library and its constituencies. Placing an advertisement in a local newspaper or on a radio or television program are examples of advertising. A popular way for organizations to be able to advertise without spending money is what is traditionally known as 'advertising trades.' A library could trade meeting space with a local radio station. The library could use radio advertising to spread the word about an upcoming program. The radio station could use library meeting space for their next off-site retreat. Using a bit of creativity and thought can save organizations quite a bit when it comes to advertising.

The best advertisements are recognized with the Clio Awards, much the way great films are awarded with an Oscar. Known for its world-class juries made up of 113 experts from 62 countries, the Clio Awards focus on creative work in the fields of advertising and design, specifically in the areas of TV, Print, Outdoor, Radio, Content and Contact, Integrated Campaign, Innovative Media, Interactive, Design and student work.[5] Information on the advertisements is posted on their website and many of the award-winning TV commercials can be viewed on websites such as YouTube.com.

Recently, nonprofit organizations have been putting a lot of money into advertising. Advertising spending by nonprofits increased to $576.5 million in 2003, up from $497.7 million in 2002 (an increase of 15.8 percent). According to the New York Times, 'Nonprofits and advocacy groups face many of the same challenges that confront corporate advertisers ... due to the deluge of come-ons directed at ever-more splintered audiences.' In the past, libraries and other nonprofits have depended on donated advertising, which, although free, comes with problems. According to Jerry Della Femina, chairman at Della Femina Rothschild Jeary & Partners, a large advertising agency in New York: 'Public service announcements basically are unfortunately the beggars of the advertising industry ... The networks put them on at 3:30 in the morning, somewhere between guys selling you knives and guys selling you dumpling makers.'[6]

Personal selling

Although libraries typically do not engage in personal selling à la the Hoover vacuum cleaner salesperson, in the most general sense personal selling is face-to-face communication between the organization and its constituencies. A library director, for example, could be said to be engaging in personal selling by soliciting additional funding from the community. A student recently told me about an experience going to her public library and being approached by the library's Friends organization. The extremely helpful Friend started a conversation with the student about becoming a member for a nominal fee, and all the benefits she could receive by signing up that day. Personal selling at its best!!

Sales promotion

Sales promotion generally consists of what many people would consider tchotskis, those nominal takeaway gifts with logos imprinted on them. Examples include library branded tote bags, T-shirts, pads, pens, etc. These takeaway 'gifts' remind patrons about the library every time they use or see another using (for example) a library tote bag. An example of a successful library promotion can be seen in Cambridge Public Library's 'Bags for Babies' campaign. Library branded tote bags containing three baby books and information on reading to children are sent to every parent of a newborn child in the Cambridge Public Library area, helping parents and babies onto the right path to reading.

Public relations

Public relations (PR) tends to be the least well understood component of the promotional mix. Many associate PR with crisis management, as when a political figure gets caught with their hand in the cookie jar – the PR person is typically seen as the 'spin doctor' that tries to put a positive perspective on the scandal. ('He was just removing the old cookies, now there are fresh cookies for us all!') Crisis management is only a small part of the activities that constitute PR. Philip Kotler, in *Kotler on Marketing: How to Create, Win, and Dominate Markets,*[7] explains the tools of PR using the 'pencils' acronym:

- Publications – organizational publications, annual reports, brochures.

- Events – sponsoring sports events, art shows, special programming.

- News – favorable stories about the library or people, usually as a result of sending out press releases.

- Community involvement activities – contributions of library resources to local community needs.

- Lobbying activity – influencing favorable or dissuading unfavorable legislation and rulings.

- Social responsibility – building a good reputation for being a good organizational citizen.[8]

Additionally, several other PR techniques also exist.[9] These include:

- *Audience targeting.* A fundamental technique used in public relations is to identify the target audience and to tailor every message to appeal to that audience. It can be a general, nationwide or worldwide audience, but it is more often a segment of a population. Marketers often refer to economy-driven 'demographics' such as 'white males 18–49,' but in public relations an audience is more fluid, being whomever someone wants to reach. For example, recent political audiences include 'soccer moms' and 'NASCAR dads.'

- *Optimized press releases.* Unlike conventional press releases of yore written for journalists' eyes only in hopes the editor or reporter would find the content compelling enough to turn it into print or electronic news coverage, the optimized press release is posted on an online news portal. Here the writer carefully selects keywords or keyword phrases relevant to the press release contents. If written skillfully, the press release can rank highly in searches on Google News, Yahoo or MSN News (or the many other minor news portals) for the chosen keyword phrases.

- *Spin.* In public relations, spin is a sometimes pejorative term signifying a heavily biased portrayal in one's own favor of an event or situation. While traditional public relations may also rely on creative presentation of the facts, 'spin' often, though not always, implies disin-genuous, deceptive and/or highly manipulative tactics.

- *Astroturfing.* This is the creation of an artificial grass-roots movement. A typical example would be the writing of letters to multiple newspaper editors under different names to express an opinion on an issue, creating the impression of widespread public feeling but one controlled by a single entity.

- *Whisper campaign.* This is a method of persuasion in which damaging rumors or innuendo are spread about the target, while the source of the rumors seeks to avoid being detected while spreading them. It also works to garner buzz about an elite product.

Public libraries in particular can benefit from PR. Techniques learned from the PR field can be applied to libraries without a PR budget. Garnering public interest can equate to more funding and higher circulation – and since part of a PR professional's job is to educate the public about an organization's mission and role in the community, together they can do great things, for example holding a 'Waived Fines Day' to attract users with guilty consciences about long overdue books and creating a positive experience by eliminating the fees. Also, hosting booths at local fairs and community events can gain positive publicity for the library. In fact, the Massachusetts Library Association hosts annual PR awards in a variety of areas including summer reading, library cards, events, etc. Winners of the awards have the upper hand in state library funding the following year.

Libraries tend to gravitate towards public relations in their marketing efforts as many of the tools (for example, writing press releases) are considered to be low-cost expenditures (as opposed to advertising). But because many media outlets will promote library events at no cost to the library, it's important to remember that they, not the library, have control over the message they send.

The following case study illustrates how the promotional mix is used at Trinity Library. Exercise 2.2 will help to get you thinking about the marketing mix at your library.

Case study 2.2

Trinity's promotional mix

While the Library uses all four parts of the promotional mix, it primarily relies on public relations and advertising to promote itself. In the public relations sector, press releases are usually issued by the College

Communications office for any exhibition or other event that is going to happen at the library. While local newspapers will usually print the events listing, they will on occasion write a feature article on the upcoming event. Examples include when the Watkinson Library celebrated its fiftieth anniversary at Trinity College in 2003 and when the College Library celebrated its one millionth volume. In any case, the press release is used to promote the Library's resources to the world outside of Trinity College. Within the College community, the two venues for public relations are the *Trinity Tripod*, which usually includes a feature article based on the press release and the advertising of the event, and the Trinity Exchange website, where a shorter version of the press release is posted for the community to read.

In addition to the articles in the *Tripod*, the Library might also place advertisements announcing the latest event. Advertising for events is usually limited to a few 11×17 posters that are designed and printed within the College and the brochure if it is an exhibit. Sometimes fliers are also used. While they were formerly placed in all student mailboxes, this activity has been curtailed in recent years and instead the fliers have been used as mailings to the Library Associates (Friends of the Library) to let them know of the events that are happening. By specifically targeting that market with advertising, the Library knows that it will gain a greater yield of people because the people on the mailing list have shown a genuine interest in events at the Library. However, it does not draw new people to events because they are unaware of the events happening.

Personal selling is achieved mostly within the College community to the two populations, faculty and students. When performing personal selling with faculty, the goal is often to talk personally with the faculty of departments that would benefit most from a particular event. Outreach Librarian Jessica Smith gives an example: 'We recently held an author talk and book signing on a timely urban issue and shared the details with faculty members from the political science, economics, sociology, and education studies departments, as well as the community learning initiative.' By specifically targeting certain professors and classes that would benefit most from a given event, the hope is that attendance will be higher because the people who would be the most interested are notified of the details. However, while faculty are often enthusiastic when they find out about events, they often do not follow up and go to events, or mandate that their students attend.

The second form of personal selling used by the Library includes bibliographic instruction and relationships built between students and the librarians. Each member of the staff is there to promote resources the College has access to, both print and digital. Aside from the general bibliographic instruction workshops given to first-year students at the beginning of the academic year, many of the bibliographic instruction workshops are tailored to a specific class and often to a specific assignment. Often a professor will ask one of the reference librarians to do a presentation highlighting the key information in a topical area and how to find it. Because each reference librarian has a relationship with a particular department, majors from the department can often build a working relationship with the librarian, who promotes the full range of the Library's services to the student, especially those relevant to the area of study. While this allows students to use the library more fully and more efficiently, it is only effective on students who already use the Library. While some bibliographic instruction workshops may be the first time students have really learned about the resources of the Library, they also have to make the step to really try to listen to the presentations offered by librarians. While this personal selling is often effective in getting students to use the Library in the short term to complete one assignment, it is not often effective in getting them to remain dedicated Library users (unless they are undertaking a long-term assignment, such as a thesis).

The only sector of the promotional mix that is severely under-utilitized by the Library is sales promotion. This could be because it does not translate well to the realm of the Library. However, the Watkinson's exhibitions could be viewed as a sales promotion because they are meant to show exhibit viewers what resources the Library has in the hopes that the viewers will decide to use more of the same resources. It is a way for a sample of the collection to be viewed by the public in an otherwise closed-stacked special collections library. Small exhibitions of some of the College Library's main collection books are also placed strategically to let the community know of new or important works. These display cases are located mostly in the pathway as one is entering the Library, both by the door and at the entrances to the reading room. However, these are not often highlighted adequately, changed regularly, or largely noticed by the general populace, and could be better utilized as a form of sales promotion.

Exercise 2.2 Identifying your library's promotional mix

Following the example in Table 2.1, fill in another similar table with your own library's marketing mix and suggestions for improving it.

Table 2.1 Cambridge Public Library's promotional mix

Mix element	How the CPL does it	Ways to make it better
Advertising	*Cambridge Chronicle*: a city-based newspaper read mainly by residents Flyers	Free advertising online and in print at Craigslist.com, Boston Calendar, Boston.com, Stuff@Night, The Metro Advertising in Spanish
Personal selling	Encouraging great customer service No dress code, which means they don't always dress to impress	Mandatory yearly Customer Service training Uniforms, a more formal dress code, or even just simple CPL polo shirts
Sales promotion	Nothing more than book displays and regular programming	Cambridge-specific library cards Waived Fines Week
Public relations	On & Off Broadway Bamboo the Panda	Put it online! Check that all flyers and notices have the library logo on it Just MORE in general!

Linking marketing with mission

It is imperative that your marketing efforts reflect the mission of the library. Most change efforts are doomed to failure if the people at the top are not supportive, and a new marketing plan is no different. Take a look at your library's mission statement. Chances are it says something about 'serving the needs of the community.' Would they be better served if they knew about the services you offer? You bet. Consider including your commitment to promoting the library's services in your mission statement, as the case studies of the libraries that follow have done. Exercises 2.3 and 2.4 will help connect your services with your library's mission and start you thinking about using the tools of the promotional mix.

Case study 2.3

The Seattle Public Library links marketing with mission

The first sentence of the Seattle Public Library's mission statement declares: 'Our mission is to become the best public library in the world by being so tuned into the people we serve and so supportive of each other's efforts that we are able to provide highly responsive service.'[10] The current 'Libraries for All' project demonstrates a commitment to responsive service, not only through building new facilities, but also hearing patron complaints on library hours and recognizing the changing needs of a diverse population. For example, world language and English as a second language materials for adults were added to collections in almost all of the libraries. The Seattle Public Library plans for change and innovation.

The staff of the Seattle Public Library do not just check in and out and shelve books; every staff member has some role in marketing the library. As the mission statement implies in its conclusion, '[we] serve our public with expert and caring assistance; and reach out to all members of our community.'[11] Marketing is integral to every job description. An example of the importance of marketing highlighted in a staff position is in the 2004 Annual Report. Chance Hunt was profiled in *Library Journal* as a 'Mover and Shaker':

> Hunt is the key liaison to the Seattle Public Schools and all other government agencies that serve kids … 'The most important thing I do is communicate the Library's mission … That way, when city officials shave the budget, they'll remember that the public library is a key part of early literacy, student achievement, and the overall quality of life.'[12]

Case study 2.4

Cambridge Public Library links marketing and mission

The Cambridge Public Library's mission statement is:

> So that enlightenment and literacy may flourish in our community, the Cambridge Public Library (CPL) dedicates itself to collecting and distributing an array of information and ideas that is diverse in material, varied in formats and rich in viewpoint, reflecting the multicultural character of the community and world it serves. The Library provides free, equal, and confidential access to its resources and services. *Essential to this mission is the active promotion of library services, collections, and programs* [emphasis added].[13]

The library in Cambridge has come up with a number of unique programs to promote its mission statement, programs that are worth advertising and promoting.

Beyond basic books, DVDs, CD, and reference services, the library offers programs such as *Cambridge Reads*, a city-wide event where everyone reads one book (for example, Khaled Hosseini's *The Kite*

Runner). The CPL hosts book talks, discussion groups and panels, and even the author for a large event. *The Literacy Project* offers free ESL groups, computer classes, and reading and writing tutorials. The Summer Reading Program (*Get Wrapped Up* – this summer's Egyptian theme – and *Stuff* for high-school students) offers promotions to get kids to read, booklists, activities, and events at the libraries across the city. The Children's Department sends Baby Bags to every parent of a newborn child with three baby books and information on reading to children, to help parents and babies get on the right path to reading. For seniors, the CPL has a volunteer who teaches a weekly exercise class and a delivery service to homebound patrons. They also have a variety of book groups at the main library and one at each branch.

Part of the library's vision states:

> Cambridge [...] envisions its public library as a doorway to opportunity, self-development and recreation for all its residents, and as a forum where they may share ideas, cultures and resources among themselves and with people around the globe. The free availability of information, the lively interaction of people, and the open exchange of ideas animate and extend the democratic traditions from which our city, our country and our people have so greatly benefited.[14]

It is interesting to compare the marketing of the CPL to its mission and vision statements. The programming partially fits this description. All of the programming is free and open to everyone, and the library does a great job providing programs and materials for a variety of interests, literacy levels and language skills. They do not, however, market to these people in the same way.

For example, 'Major languages and language groups recorded in Cambridge in 2000 include Spanish (5.2 percent), French, including Haitian Creole (4.6 percent), Chinese (4.0 percent) and Portuguese (3.2 percent). In 1999, public school families spoke over 60 different languages at home.'[15] Virtually none of the flyers are done in Spanish (starting in summer 2007 CPL will have a Circulation Policies and

Procedures notice available in Spanish). Not even the ESL conversation group advertisements are in Spanish. The literacy programs to teach English speakers to read and write are created in simple formats, but still primarily made up of words. If you cannot read a sign, you cannot learn about the classes available – period. Advertising online for the computer classes will not help someone who cannot even turn on a computer. In 2000, 26,218 residents – 25.9 percent – were foreign born, including 8,283 naturalized citizens.[16] There has to be away to connect with these people, many of whom might not have any idea what the library can offer.

Exercise 2.3   **Connecting marketing to mission**

Select a user group (for example, reference, children's programming, an annual event, preschoolers, non-English speaking users, or retirees). Describe how the marketing of this service or to this group will contribute to the library's mission. For instance, if part of the mission of your library is to serve the community, then say that marketing will let the community know how you can serve them.

Exercise 2.4   **Promotion**

Discuss how your library could use the following:

- Collateral materials
  (i.e. bumper stickers,
  bookmarks, buttons) ————————————————
- Annual report ——————————————————————
- New releases ———————————————————————
- News memo for
  quick release ————————————————————————
- Brochures ——————————————————————————

- Direct mail————————————————————————————
- Newsletters————————————————————————————
- Special event —————————————————————————
- Feature story —————————————————————————
- Press kit ———————————————————————————
- Photographs ————————————————————————
- Posters ——————————————————————————
- Public service announcements —————————————————
- Speeches/public appearances ——————————————————

Notes

1. Philip Kotler (2002) *Strategic Marketing for Nonprofit Organizations*, 6th edn. Englewood Cliffs, NJ: Prentice Hall, p. 8.
2. Ibid.
3. Attributed to General Eric Shinseki, Chief of Staff, US Army, as quoted by Tom Peters (2003) *Re-imagine!* London: DK Ltd.
4. See: *http://www.maine.gov/msl/services/calculator.htm* (accessed 17 July 2007).
5. See: *http://www.clioawards.com/press/index.cfm* (accessed 17 July 2007).
6. Nat Ives (2004) 'Advertising: to get their messages across, more and more nonprofit organizations are going commercial,' *New York Times*, 20 February.
7. Philip Kotler (1999) *Kotler on Marketing: How to Create, Win, and Dominate Markets*. New York: Free Press.
8. Ibid.
9. See:*http://en.wikipedia.org/wiki/Public_relations#Methods.2C_tools.2C_and_tactics* (accessed 17 July 2007).
10. See: *http://www.spl.org/default.asp?pageID=about_mission* (accessed 17 July 2007).
11. Ibid.

12. Seattle Public Library (2005) *Annual Report*, p. 16.
13. Cambridge Public Library Mission Statement, available at: *http://www.ci.cambridge.ma.us/%7ECPL/about/mission.html* (accessed 17 July 2007).
14. Cambridge Public Library Vision Statement, available at: *http://www.cambridgema.gov/CPL/about/strategicplan.html* (accessed 17 July 2007).
15. Cambridge Public Library Census Data, available at: *http://www.cambridgema.gov/~CDD/data/datafaq.html#1* (accessed 17 July 2007).
16. Ibid.

3

Innovation 101

Introduction

In the first chapter of this text, we discussed why libraries need to be innovative and market themselves. This chapter will discuss what innovation is and how both businesses and libraries are being innovative.

What is innovation?

Innovation is the managed effort of an organization to develop new products and services or new uses for existing products and services. It can also include marketing a product in a new way or to a different target market. Innovation can be radical or incremental, technical or managerial, product or process.

Radical innovations are new products, services or technologies that completely replace the existing items in the market. For example, compact disks have replaced vinyl records, DVDs are replacing VCRs and iPods are replacing Walkmans. *Incremental innovations* modify existing products, services, and technologies. Consumers have become accustomed to dependable products and now look for faster, smaller, lighter, and brighter products. These features are sometimes referred to as 'bells and whistles'; however, there are segments of the market that live for these types of innovations. An example of an incremental innovation can be seen in the cell phone market. Cell phones can now be used as digital cameras and can include unique ring tones, games, and many other features.

Technical innovations are changes to a product, service, or technology that involves the way the item is produced. Examples include the vacuum tube being replaced by the transistor and the integrated circuit being replaced by the microchip. *Managerial innovations* are changes in the way which products and services are conceived, built, and delivered to customers. Examples of managerial innovation include outsourcing and re-engineering.

Product innovations are changes in the physical characteristics or performance of existing products and services, or the creation of brand new services. An example of a product innovation can be seen in the personal digital assistant replacing diaries and calculators and online air reservations replacing travel agencies. *Process innovations* are changes in the way products or services are manufactured, created, or distributed. Japanese organizations have excelled at process innovation. An example of this distinction can be seen in their manufacturing processes for cars and cameras – Japanese firms invest in their process technology to find better ways to produce products with fewer steps, lower costs, and less waste.

The state of management innovation

Many people feel that the pace of truly innovative developments has declined alarmingly in organizations, particularly when compared with our foreign competitors.

Organizations fail to innovate for at least three reasons: lack of resources, failure to recognize opportunities, and resistance to change.

Lack of resources

Innovation is expensive for companies in terms of time, money, and energy. If the firm does not have the resources in terms of the kinds of employees it needs to be innovative, or sufficient funds to champion a program of innovation, it may fall behind in developing innovative products and services. An example of this can be seen in Hewlett-Packard not investing in Apple computer's original idea for a personal computer due its many other commitments in the electronic instruments and computer industry. If HP had more financial resources, they may have entered this market early and had a head start on the competition.

Failure to recognize opportunities

Due to the fact that organizations cannot pursue all good ideas, they must develop a screening process to carefully evaluate new innovations and select the ones that hold the greatest potential. If organizations are not skilled at recognizing and evaluating opportunities, they may be overly cautious and fail to invest in innovations that turn out to be successful for other firms. One of the best known examples of this is that of Xerox and the graphical user interface (GUI). Xerox developed the GUI at its lab in Palo Alto, California but failed to see the opportunities associated with it. It took Steve Jobs of Apple computer on a visit to the lab to realize the tremendous potential of this innovation and incorporate it into a remarkable product – the Apple Macintosh.

Resistance to change

Many organizations resist innovation because it means changing the old ways of doing things in favor of new products and new ways of doing things. This can be personally difficult for employees and managers, thus this resistance can slow down the innovation process. A prime example of this is the QWERTY keyboard. This keyboard was invented for the typewriter and designed so that the keys next to each other would not jam. Subsequent better designs such as the DVORAK keyboard made typing faster and less stressful on the hands. But typewriter companies, keyboard manufacturers, and typing teachers fought the change. Today we still type on the QWERTY keyboard and have carpel tunnel syndrome, showing that vested interests can set up barriers to thwart innovative designs.

Case study 3.1

3M

Not surprisingly, the 3M Company has a long history of encouraging intra-preneurship. Intrapreneurship is the manifestation of innovation within an established business structure. Employees are given a chance to see if their ideas work by spending company time and resources while exploring their new product ideas. 'Seeing what works' presumes that many of their ideas will not work. Visionary companies like 3M tend to have a much higher tolerance for innovative failure. The intrapreneur's road to success will be accompanied by many mistakes, but innovative companies realize that these mistakes can lead to great successes. Just look at the ubiquit-ous Post-It notes, first deemed to be a failure as the glue 'did not stick.'

3M has also created an award for libraries. It is sponsored by 3M New Zealand Limited in conjunction with the Library and Information Association of New Zealand Aotearoa to 'promote excellence and innovation in Library and Information services.' [1] The award is given to the librarian, information specialist or team who has applied an innovative and entrepreneurial approach to their business. The prizes are $4,000 for the winner, $1,000 for second place, and $500 of 3M products for third place. The money awarded to first and second place is to be used for professional development. Table 3.1 shows the winners of the awards since its inception in 1996.

Table 3.1   **Recipients of 3M Library Award for Innovation in Libraries**

1996	Information Services – Special Education Service Cost-effective CD-ROM Database Distribution project
1997	Hama Whakapapa Restoration and Research Database project
1998	Auckland War Memorial Museum Library Cenotaph database project
1999	Christchurch College of Education NZEdSearch
2000	Horowhenua Library Trust Koha – a free library web-based database
2001	Southland Boys' High School Real Men Read Books: *http://www.edgazette.govt.nz/ articles/show_articles.php?id=6080*
2002	Manukau City Libraries Tupu – Dawson Road Youth Library project
2003	Parliamentary Library Infocus
2004	Taranaki Information Network Puke Ariki
2005	AnyQuestions National Library with Auckland, Wellington, Christchurch and Manukau Public Libraries
2006	eLGAR – Auckland City, Waitakere, Rodney, North Shore and Manukau Libraries Smarter Systems Project*

* See *http://www.lianza.org.nz/about/awards/industry.html#3m* (accessed 27 July 2007).

Case study 3.2

Sundance Film Institute

In a nation where so many projects and products fail, 35 percent of projects developed in the filmmakers Sundance Lab and 85 percent of its Theater Lab projects make it to production – this means that more than 85 feature films have been produced in 22 years. The brand is so well recognized that it has become shorthand for independent filmmaking. And there's a Sundance shelf in more than 4,000 Blockbuster stores. Also affiliated with Sundance is the Sundance channel, which now has more than 16.7 million subscribers.

These successful innovations come from Robert Redford's unshakable belief that growth is not an accounting practice, but a creative process, not just for companies in the entertainment industry, but for ordinary companies that produce toilet paper, wallets, and fertilizer.

Sundance is the purest example of sustained innovation and creative culture found in organizations today. The key to a constantly innovating organization is a constantly innovating founder. Redford created the Sundance Institute, in part, to combat the deadening reputation that he saw stifling the film industry. But it was his instincts for nurturing creativity in others that made it thrive. Company leaders – particularly the founder and keeper of the vision – can set the tone for how employees behave toward one another. The tone Redford has set is one of generosity. This kind of generosity sets the table for collaboration.

Innovation in companies is pursued with desperate, random acts, or unevolved strategies. Or it is so incremental and predictable that it is not really innovation at all. Sundance, by contrast, doesn't just encourage innovation – it ensures that it happens by process and design. People are exposed to a variety of conflicting perspectives. Allowances are made for experimentation, mistakes, and dead ends. They engage in conversations that lead to new conclusions rather than persuading them of foregone ones. They don't respond slavishly to market research ... and their leader gives generously of his time and his attention to innovators.[2]

Create a 'purple cow'

In Seth Godin's book *The Purple Cow*, he states that organizations need to be innovative by creating truly remarkable products and services and marketing them to the right group of people. He also discusses the way that the marketing of innovative products has changed. He states that the old rule for marketing new products was to 'create safe, ordinary products and combine them with great marketing.' The new rule is to 'create remarkable products that the right people seek out.'[3]

The idea behind Godin's book is that 'something remarkable is worth talking about. Worth noticing. Exceptional. New. Interesting. It's a purple cow. Boring stuff is invisible. It's a brown cow.'[4]

Godin states:

> I don't think there's a shortage of remarkable ideas. I think that your business has plenty of great opportunities to do great things. Nope, what's missing isn't the ideas. It's the will to execute them.[5]

Tom Peters echoes this sentiment in *The Pursuit of Wow!* He believes that the only way to accomplish change is to DO it. He states: 'In short, you do it and it's done. Then you work like hell for the rest of your life to stay on the ... bandwagon.' In short, if your organization is committed to being innovative, start this second and keep at it every day. Peters uses the analogy of being on a diet or joining AA. 'The decision is not the hard part, but it's maintaining the commitment to it every single day that is.'[6] Purple cows will be discussed further in Chapter 5.

Lessons from bookstores

In a recent article, Chris Rippel discusses what libraries can learn from bookstores. Rippel invites librarians to study and apply techniques bookstores use to communicate with customers so that librarians can communicate better with their patrons. He identifies smell, music, and lighting, which make up a category known as retail atmospherics, and other items such as signage, book and lighting displays. He also discusses how libraries have used 'bookstore-like' lighting displays to attract patrons to the new arrivals shelf.[7]

The stickiness factor

According to Malcolm Gladwell's best selling book *The Tipping Point*, in order for a product to be a successful innovation, it has to have what he calls 'stickiness.' Stickiness refers to the way information about the product is disseminated to the market. He states that there is a simple way to package information that, under the right circumstances, can make the product irresistible. All a company needs to do is find it. He acknowledges that large amounts of repetitive advertising can work (along with the large sums of money needed to support it) but that there are other smaller, subtler, and easier ways to make something work.[8] Seth Godin calls these small ideas 'soft innovations.' Chapter 5 explores soft innovations further.

Made to stick

In their book *Made to Stick*, Chip and Dan Heath explore Gladwell's 'stickiness factor' to try to determine why some ideas stick in our memories and others do not. They boil down their ideas to six factors which make up the acronym 'success' (well, sort of).

- *Simple*. Each idea should be stripped down to its core so that the main points stand out. The authors use Southwest's commitment to being *the* 'low-cost air carrier' as an example. Every new idea is evaluated against 'Will it help us to achieve our goal of being *the* low-cost airline?' If yes, it goes forward; if not, the idea gets tossed out.

- *Unexpected*. The idea must be surprising in some respect and destroy our preconceived notions about it. One example used is the 'Jared Subway Sandwich' commercials. Jared lost a ton of weight by eating Subway subs. You don't usually expect that a fast-food restaurant will help you *lose* weight ... therefore, the unexpected comes into play.

- *Concrete*. Ideas that are concrete use real-world analogies and avoid using statistics. The authors use an example of giving to charities as an example – charitable appeals that use large numbers to communicate the magnitude of a problem are less effective than using a single person that is affected by the problem.

- *Credible.* This component has to do with trusting the sender of the message. To illustrate again with the Jared Subway promotion, Jared created the subway diet plan – not some big government agency that's telling you what to eat, how much to eat, and when to eat it.

- *Emotional.* Information makes people think, emotion makes them act. This concept can again be illustrated through the charitable appeal example – one person's suffering elicits an emotional response from us and we are much more likely to contribute to charities that touch our emotions.

- *Story.* Stories tend to connect people and make them pay closer attention to what your ideas are. Jared's weight loss was a great story – overcoming a huge obstacle by doing a few simple things.[9]

Exercise 3.1   **Make it stick**

Examine your library's marketing messages – do they fit the SUCCESS test for stickiness? If not, how can you change them so they do?

Innovative libraries

Many libraries have been noted for being innovative. Once such library is the Ferguson Library in Stamford, Connecticut. In the age before libraries were actively implanting cafés, the Ferguson Library added a 1,700 square foot Starbucks onto the library property, making it the second library in the Untied States with a Starbucks on the premises. Additionally, the Ferguson Library started offering passport photo services at the library and eventually expanded its passport services due to the demand for them. Ferguson is also noted for its innovative programming.

Another innovative library is the Salt Lake City Library. In addition to the magnificent building (see *http://www .slcpl.lib.ut.us/details.jsp?parent_id=7&page_id=5*), the library also has a large mall inside. Retailers include The Library Store, The English Garden, The Salt Lake Roasting Company, and many others.

Exercise 3.2   **Brainstorm**

Take out a pad of paper and write down as many thoughts as you can for innovative ways to attract people to your library. Give yourself 15 minutes, and do not try to critique the ideas as you write them down. Remember, the sky is the limit here – don't think of resource constraints or get bogged down thinking 'we could never do that here.'

When your 15 minutes are up, compare your list to the list that follows (compiled from library marketing seminars). Which ones can you implement right away?

'Remarkable' ideas for libraries

- E-mail patrons journal articles, chapters from books of interest (à la Amazon)
- Childcare with programming for holiday shoppers
- Delivery of hot food and books after 6 p.m.
- Coupons from local stores
- 'Peapod' for books
- Sponsor a stack

- Singles party
- Oxygen bar
- Singles movie night
- Spa night
- Curbside pickup for books
- Drive thru
- Children's programs at grocery store
- Adult programs with story time
- Historical/musical character's series
- 'Thunderstorm Thursdays'
- Rock wall in children's room
- 'Tappas Tuesdays'

Notes

1. See: *http://www.lianza.org.nz/about/awards/industry.html #3m* (accessed 27 July 2007).
2. Stephen Zades (2003) 'Creativity regained,' *Inc. Magazine*, 25 September, p. 9.
3. Seth Godin (2003) *Purple Cow – Transform Your Business by Being Remarkable*. New York: Penguin Group.
4. Ibid.
5. Ibid
6. Tom Peters (1994) *The Pursuit of Wow! Every Person's Guide to Topsy-Turvy Times*. New York: Vintage Books.
7. Chris Rippel (2007) 'What libraries can learn from bookstores: applying bookstore design to public libraries,' *LYP Online In Focus Special Report*, 2 February. Available at: *http://www.lyponline.com/infocus/In_Focus.htm* (accessed 28 January 2008).
8. Malcolm Gladwell (2000) *The Tipping Point – How Little Things Can Make a Big Difference*. New York: Little, Brown.

9. Chip and Dan Heath (2007) *Made to Stick: Why Some Ideas Survive and Others Die*. New York: Random House.

4

Trends

Introduction

In order to create library products and services that our customers will seek out, it is necessary to have some understanding of the trends that affect the lives of our patrons.

One of the best selling authors on the subject of trends is Faith Popcorn. Popcorn's book *The Popcorn Report* and her later book *Clicking* identify several trends that continue to evolve in the lives of consumers. 'But aren't trends really just fads that will be over by the time this book makes it into print?' I'm often asked. No, they are not. According to Popcorn, 'A fad is a flash in the pan, a quick trick you can turn to make your money and run. Pogs were a fad.'[1] Too many pogs were produced to be collectable and kids got sick of them after a short time, like many other products in the kiddy consumer market (beanie babies, cabbage patch dolls, furbies, etc. come to mind). Trends, on the other hand, 'are what drives consumers to buy products. Trends are big and broad. Although they start small ... scattered here and there, they have a way of gaining strength.'[2] Popcorn identified 17 trends in her book *Clicking*. They are also described on her website *http://www.faithpopcorn.com*. Seven of these trends are: cocooning, clanning, fantasy adventure, small indulgences, anchoring, 99 lives, and cashing out.

Cocooning

In *The Popcorn Report*, cocooning is described as the need to make our homes into a cozy retreat.[3] Popcorn predicted the rise of home delivery businesses and home entertainment centers. Due to anxiety about crime and violence, this trend has evolved from living in our homes and being 'snug as a bug in a rug' to being as 'scared as a hare in a chair.' We have gone from our homes being home sweet home to home safe home. The increase in the number of home security systems (one in every three homes built has one), gas masks, etc., illustrates how this trend has manifested itself.

As an example the seating area at the Plaistow Public Library in Plaistow, New Hampshire, illustrates how libraries can use the cocooning trend (see Figure 4.1). A big comfortable sofa and closed seating arrangement allows people to have the comforts of home at their library.

Clanning

In *Clicking*, Popcorn describes clanning as what 'links us up with others who share our interests, ideas and aspirations.' 'I'm part of a group, and proud of it. I belong.' [4] Popcorn states that clanning examples can be found in all levels of society and 'range from the sublime to the ridiculous.' They can be 'political, economic, communal, spiritual or virtual in nature. They can have 20 members or 20,000.'[5] Examples of clans include fraternities, book clubs,

Figure 4.1 The seating area at the Plaistow Public Library in Plaistow, NH

Parrottheads, AA members, and so on. According to Popcorn, 'A clannish feeling is being recaptured at both mega-bookstores and strong independents. They have become communal hangouts for those who want to identify themselves as book lovers and sensitive individuals.' One such bookstore uses overstuffed chairs, wood shelves, and plush carpeting that create a 'warm and welcoming space where patrons can enjoy poetry readings while sipping on coffee and nibbling on pastries.'[6] Popcorn also states, 'It feels like a safe haven because you can be nearly certain that everyone is reasonably literate, intelligent, and shares a love for books and browsing.' She further describes one bookstore in New York City which 'has become a popular place to meet suitable dates – many people would rather begin a relationship with a quiet chat than the tipsy blather common in singles bars.'[7]

An example of this can be seen at the Plaistow Public Library. Girls participate in the NH Traveling Pants Program (see Figure 4.2), allowing them to 'clan' through their familiarity with the Sisterhood of the Traveling Pants best seller. (More information is available at: *http://www. flickr.com/photos/nhtravelingpants/.*)

Figure 4.2 Participation in the Traveling Pants Program, Plaistow Public Library, NH

Fantasy adventure

According to Popcorn, fantasy adventure is 'about seeking thrills and chills in small doses. It's about veering off the beaten path without getting too close to the edge. We want adventure and excitement – as long as we can still get to bed by 11 p.m.'[8] Popcorn states that most of us live pretty mundane lives, filled with routine and stress. We desire to be lifted out of this situation, albeit temporarily, to something more magical. Fantasy adventure does not necessarily mean that you have to book a cruise or even leave your home. Popcorn states that you can participate in fantasy adventure through something as simple as eating exotic food. She cites the explosion of exotic foods in the supermarket and growth of ethnic restaurants. Food isn't the only way we participate in fantasy adventure; Popcorn also points to buying from the J. Peterman catalog, exotic movies and films, Range Rovers, superstores like those of the Virgin Group and the Bass Pro Shops, amusement parks, the sport of orienteering ... and the list goes on. Anything that allows us to escape (safely) and return (eventually) can be considered to be part of this trend.

The Plaistow Public Library uses the trend of fantasy adventure though its Summer Reading Program (see Figure 4.3). The pirate theme was used throughout the library –

Figure 4.3   **Summer Reading Program, Plaistow Public Library, NH**

New Hampshire Summer Reading Program 2006

children received 'pirate booty' for reading books which could be exchanged for prizes in the library. The theme included pirate cooking lessons in which library users could learn to make 'tack' and other pirate delicacies.

Small indulgences

Popcorn's trend of small indulgences is about 'treating yourself well and not busting the bank in the process.'[9] Popcorn argues that we grew up thinking that the quality of life would improve from generation to generation, and we would experience the luxuries that our parents never had, but 'without warning, the rules changed and the promise was broken, smashed into the garbage heap.'[10] These days, we work more hours and enjoy our lives less. We have no promise of job security, and have difficulty scraping up cash needed for a down payment on a house. To combat this stress, Popcorn says that we turn to mini-luxuries to make ourselves feel better. 'They don't solve anything, but they make us feel pampered and a little bit rich for a brief, but refreshing, moment.'[11] Popcorn cites items such as food, for example fresh squeezed orange juice, fountain pens exceeding $50, back rubs, gourmet coffee and teas, flowers ... even doggie mouthwash to pamper our pooches!

Anchoring

Popcorn describes anchoring as consumers looking for what was comforting and valuable to them in the past in order to be secure in the future. In order to do this, people reach back to their roots, including religion, to ground themselves. She points to the growth of yoga and meditation and people turning back to their religious roots. She argues: 'Church attendance is soaring – more people attend church than all sporting events combined. Megachurches sometimes have to rent the nearest stadium to hold the thousands of faithful who come for Easter Sunday service.'[12] She also cites the growing number of people that believe in astrology and angels as being part of this trend. Popcorn states that the common thread through these examples is that 'we are all searching for meaning that transcends the corporeal, the material, the temporary.'[13]

99 lives

99 lives is that trend that revolves around the 'idea that we have too little time, too many responsibilities and not enough of ourselves to spread around.'[14] Technological gadgets such as pocket organizers, recorders, and cell phones all help us to manage our lives that go at breakneck speeds. Fast food has become faster and many traditionally sit-down restaurants (Chilis, Applebees, Outback, and the like) now offer curbside pickup. Popcorn also discusses the backlash to the 99 lives trend – that there is a distinct undercurrent of a retaliation to this trend. She states: 'Don't you ever feel like screaming at the endless litany of call-waiting interruptions and faxes and e-mails? The arrival of still another magazine, newsletter or catalog can make us want to light an information bonfire. The communication avalanche is adding to the stress of trying to simultaneously live 99 lives.'[15] Popcorn cites gimmicks like the 'Gotta Go' call waiting imitator, which makes a noise like the phone company's sound, but it's under your control. So if you can't get the person to stop yacking, you can hit a button and

pretend that you have to answer the call on the other line! A great time saver for those of us that have friends, co-workers (even mothers!) that are difficult to get off the phone (or don't believe that you actually 'work' from home). The next trend details this backlash in greater detail.

Cashing out

Cashing out is the trend that describes our search for a more fulfilling, simpler way of life. Popcorn gives the hypothetical example of a stressed-out top executive that leaves his briefcase in his out basket one day, and then months later emerges making goat cheese in Vermont. She states that this trend is the opposite of the Yuppie trend of the 1980s where dreams were 'epitomized by more, bigger, better, and faster.' We have learned that the quality of life has more to do with enjoying what we are doing more than what we are educated to do or the size of our paychecks. Popcorn gives numerous examples of doctors, advertising executives, computer technicians, and average people who traded in their fast-paced lives in order to do something they loved. She cites the emergence of 'business commandos' who 'build businesses in their own terms and work by a new set of rules.'[16] The spike in the growth of home-based businesses is also attributed to this trend, as well as the number of organizations, including banks, that cater to this movement.

Trends from the library world

Darlene Weingand also discusses trends in her book *Marketing/Planning Library and Information Services*. She states: 'The proactive library embraces change and the opportunities that are inevitably presented. In such a dynamic environment, the library becomes a learning organization purposefully reinventing itself to meet present and anticipated customer needs.'[17] Some of the categories of changes she cites that will impact libraries include: home, family and education, leisure and socializing, health and wellness, and economy and technology. It is interesting to note that many of these trends are similar to Popcorn's noted above.

- *Home.* Weingand suggests that changes in the home will impact libraries. Some of the changes we may see include 'virtual aquariums or scenic vistas,' along with 'soundproofed rooms.' Both of these ideas are similar to Popcorn's 99 lives trend.

- *Family and education.* Weingand states that 'Nannycams' hidden inside of teddy bears and ankle and wrist monitors for kids may become popular. This idea is similar to what Popcorn writes about cocooning. Additionally, Weingand predicts that spirituality-based camps and clubs will impact libraries, which parallels Popcorn's anchoring trend.

- *Leisure and socializing.* Weingand suggests that 'Computer-generated friendship circles [that] ... identify people around the world ... share[ing] common interests' will affect libraries. This trend corresponds with Popcorn's clanning trend.

- *Health and wellness.* 'Nutrition-on-wheels' ... delivery of an assortment of nutritious frozen meals to busy households once a week' is a trend that is related to Popcorn's 99 lives, as well as cocooning.

- *Economy and technology.* 'Packaged holidays ... hiring entrepreneurs to decorate ... packaged holiday meals ...

and personal shoppers' also relate to Popcorn's 99 lives trend.

Weingand also discusses the importance of how information is accessed and suggests that libraries should: 'Make speed your mind set,' 'Connect everything,' 'Build product into every service ... put service into every product,' and 'Put your offer online.'[18]

Exercise 4.1   Trends

Choose three of Faith Popcorn's trends and create a new library service, or discuss how an existing library product or service corresponds with each trend.

Notes

1. Faith Popcorn (1992) *The Popcorn Report*. New York: Harper Business, p. 11.
2. Ibid.
3. Ibid.
4. Faith Popcorn (1997) *Clicking: 17 Trends That Drive Your Business – And Your Life*. New York: HarperCollins, p. 46.
5. Ibid., p. 47.
6. Ibid., p. 55.
7. Ibid., p. 56.
8. Ibid., p. 59.
9. Ibid., p. 93.
10. Ibid., p. 94
11. Ibid.
12. Ibid., p. 114.
13. Ibid., p. 126.
14. Ibid., p. 199.
15. Ibid., p. 210.
16. Ibid., p. 223.

17. Darlene Weingand (1999) *Marketing/Planning Library and Information Services*, 2nd edn. Englewood, CO: Libraries Unlimited, p. 158.
18. Ibid.

Purple cows, free prizes, and Moogle, oh my!

Introduction

Seth Godin has written some pretty interesting stuff on marketing. His book *Purple Cow* discusses how organizations need to be remarkable to stand out from the competition.[1] In *Free Prize Inside*, Godin discusses how the old ways of marketing don't work anymore, and the only way to attract customers is to offer something small, yet precious – a 'free prize' – that makes it irresistible.[2] Godin has also recently published an e-book, *99 Cows*.[3] As you might have guessed, the e-book contains stories of 99 remarkable companies (OK, and a bonus 100th cow ... or would that be a free prize?). Each page has a web link from the content on the page to the organization that is being discussed. One link is to a page on his website which is a parody of Google. 'Moogle' combines Google's look, but with cow links and links which can be used to buy Godin's book.[4] Very clever. This chapter will discuss how you can create a 'Purple Owl' for your library.

Don't have a cow, man, have a Purple Cow!

In his book *Purple Cow* Seth Godin puts across that a fundamental change has occurred in the marketplace. The idea is that organizations need to create a 'Purple Cow' or something that makes their product or service remarkable in order to have their marketing message heard by their customers. In the past, organizations would simply throw money into TV ads and people would seek out their products. This is not the case anymore; according to Godin the old rule was to 'Create safe, ordinary products and combine them with great marketing.' The new rule is this: 'Create remarkable products [or services] that the right people seek out.' [5] So why don't all organizations have Purple Cows?

Godin believes the reason why most organizations don't create remarkable products and services is actually due to fear. He states: 'Some folks would like you to believe that there are too few great ideas or that their product or industry or company can't support a great idea. This, of course, is nonsense.'[6]

According to Godin, if your organization creates remarkable products, there is a chance that someone will not like you ... which is part of the definition of remarkable. Criticism inevitably comes to those who stand out. Additionally, he states, most of us believe criticism inevitably leads to failure. Godin takes the opposite view; he believes that creating products and services that don't stand out from the pack leads to failure – in essence 'being safe is risky,' and the only way to create remarkable products and services is to set them up for some serious criticism.

Godin discuses our aversion to criticism by stating that when we get it, we usually respond to it by hiding, 'avoiding the negative feedback and thus (ironically) guaranteeing that we won't succeed.' He further states: 'It's people who have projects that are never criticized who ultimately fail.' So in order to be successful, Godin believes that organizations need to create a Purple Cow. Is your Purple Cow guaranteed to work? Absolutely not! As Godin writes, 'If it was easy to be a rock star, everyone would be one! ... It's the unpredictability of the outcome that makes it work.'[7] 'Boring is always the most risky strategy. Smart business people realize this, and they work to minimize the risk from the process. They know that sometimes it's not going to work, but they accept the fact that that's okay.'[8]

Godin pushes this idea by using the example of the J. Peterman catalog. The writing in the catalog was so over the top that Peterman became a character on Seinfeld. He then compares the Peterman catalog with LL Bean or Land's End's catalog. Could it happen with one of them? Not likely.[9]

Exercise 5.1	Spoof the library

How could you modify your library's services so that you'd show up on the next Saturday Night Live, or be spoofed in a trade journal?

Are your library services very good?

Godin believes that the opposite of remarkable is not bad, but very good.[10] Jim Collins echoes this sentiment in his book *Good to Great*. The book opens with this paragraph:

> Good is the enemy of great. And that is one of the key reasons why we have so little that becomes great. We

don't have great schools, principally because we have good schools. We don't have great government, principally because we have good government. Few people attain great lives, in large part because it is just so easy to settle for a good life. The vast majority of companies never become great, precisely because the vast majority become quite good – and that is their main problem.[11]

Collins continues by showing how various companies in various organizations went beyond good and achieved greatness.

Godin illustrates the problem with 'good' through the following example:

If you travel on an airline and they get you there safely, you don't tell anyone. That's what's supposed to happen. What makes it remarkable is if [...] the service is so unexpected (they were an hour early! They served flaming crepes suzette in first class!) that you need to share it.[12]

Are your patrons getting what they expect when they come to your library? How can you make their experience remarkable?

The US Postal Service

OK, you may be thinking that your library isn't innovative and never will be. Libraries just don't innovate, you say. What about the United States Postal Service (USPS), a large government monopoly that's lumbered along since the Pony Express? Think about it.

In *Purple Cow*, Seth Godin writes that the USPS has had a very hard time innovating, as it is dominated by conservative, big customers, and most individuals are in no hurry to change their mailing habits. He states that the lion's share of new policy proposals at the Postal Service are either ignored or met with contempt, but one such initiative, ZIP+4, was a resounding success. Within a few years, the Postal Service disseminated a new idea, resulting in the change of billions of address records in thousands of databases.

Here's why it worked. The USPS created a game-changing innovation because ZIP+4 makes it much easier for marketers to target neighborhoods and makes it much faster and easier to deliver the mail. The product changed the way people deal with bulk mail as well. The USPS also singled out a few champions in organizations that were technically savvy and very sensitive to speed and price.

Godin states:

> The lesson here is simple. The more intransigent your market, the more crowded the marketplace, the busier your customers, the more you need a Purple Cow. Half measures will fail. Overhauling the product with dramatic improvements in things the right customers care about on the other hand can have a huge payoff.[13]

The Ferguson Library in Stamford, Connecticut created a Purple Cow in their library by offering passport photo services. Many libraries are offering coffee to full service cafés. The Salt Lake City Library has 20,000 square feet of retail space in their library. How can you create a Purple Owl for yours?

Otaku

Otaku is a Japanese word that describes something that's more than a hobby but a little less than an obsession. In *Purple Cow*, Seth Godin states that *otaku* is the overwhelming desire that gets someone to drive across town to try a new product in the category of interest. For example, Godin states that there are a great deal of people with a hot sauce *otaku* in the US. For example: *Blind Betty's Caribbean Hot Sauce, Lawyer's Breath, So Sue Me, Butt Burner, Spicy Chit, Habby Neros' Slap Your Mamma, Hellfire and Damnation* ... you get the point. Catsup does not have an *otaku* – you usually do not request a different variety of catsup when you go to a restaurant. However, catsup is the best selling condiment in the US – Europeans are famous for making fun of the 'ugly Americans' that destroy their culinary creations by pouring catsup over everything they eat. There are very few people by comparison that enjoy the fiery pain that various body parts endure from consuming a habañero pepper sauce, yet hot sauce has an *otaku* and catsup does not.

Godin suggests going to a science fiction convention. He states: 'Those are some pretty odd folks. Do you appeal to an audience as wacky and wonderful as this one? How could you create one?'[14] What can you add to your library programs and services to create *otaku*?

The problem with compromise

Godin states: 'The old saying is right: "a camel is a horse designed by a committee."' If the goal of marketing is to create a Purple Cow, and the nature is to be extreme in some attribute, it's inevitable that compromise can only diminish your chances of success. He says: 'If someone in your organization is charged with creating a Purple Cow, leave them alone!' Pick the right maverick and get out of their way.[15] Do you need seven levels of approval to get a new program underway? How can you pare this down?

Is your library more boring than salt?

In *Purple Cow*, Seth Godin writes that the Morton Salt Company, which has been making boring salt for over 50 years, must truly be an example of an industry where no Purple Cow can exist. If you agree, you would be wrong. Godin cites the people who make handmade salt from seawater in France that get $20 a pound for their incredible salt. The Hawaiians are creating a stir in gourmet restaurants since they recently entered the salt market. He also states 'ordinarily boring Diamond Kosher salt is looking at millions of dollars in increased annual sales because their salt tastes better on food.'[16] Additionally, the Ritz-Carlton in Amelia Island, Florida has a five-star restaurant that is named 'Salt.' It features several different types of salt that bring out the best flavor in various foods.

Other thoughts: Seth Godin says to think small. He says that the TV industrial complex has trained us to think big. 'If it doesn't appeal to everyone, the thinking goes, it's not worth it. No longer.' His advice is to think of the smallest conceivable market and create products and services that overwhelm it with its remarkability, and to 'go from there.'[17]

Other advice:

- outsource;
- copy from another industry;

- find things that 'just aren't done in libraries' and do them;
- ask 'why not?'[18]

Exercise 5.2   Make your library more exciting than salt

So do you still think your library is more boring than salt? Come up with a list of ten ways to change the services (not the hype) your library offers to make it appeal to a small sliver of your market.

Where is your library's free prize?

In the prologue of Seth Godin's *Free Prize Inside,* he states: 'Every product and every service can be remarkable. And anyone in your organization can make it happen.' The premise behind the book is the 'soft innovations' – what Godin describes as

> the clever, insightful, useful, small ideas ... that make your product into a Purple Cow; they make it remarkable. They do this by solving a problem that is peripheral to what your product is ostensibly about. It's a second reason to buy the thing, and perhaps a first reason to talk about it. It may seem like a gimmick, but soon what seems like a gimmick becomes an essential element in your product or service.[19]

He argues that the revenue associated with the soft innovation (a.k.a. 'free prize') is far greater than the cost of implementing it – good news for libraries that traditionally have had little or no money for marketing.

Additionally Godin states, 'if it satisfies consumers and gets them to tell other people what you want them to tell other people, it's not a gimmick. It's a soft innovation.'[20]

Godin believes that anyone in the organization can come up with soft innovations, but the real problem in implementing them is getting the organization to embrace the idea. In order to do this, the organization needs a champion for the new idea to see it through.

Godin also argues that innovation is actually cheaper than advertising. 'When the marketing is built into the product, creating products that are innovative is actually cheaper than advertising average products.'[21] He uses various examples to illustrate this point. One is that of Amazon.com. Amazon decided early on not to advertise, but instead to put their advertising dollars into creating free shipping for its customers. This tactic has worked out very well for Amazon and other dot coms are following their lead.

Another soft innovation Godin discusses is that of the paperback book. This simple idea, created by Robert de Graff sixty years ago, was met with a huge amount of resistance from the publishing industry. The public loved the idea and it led to billions of books being sold. Godin also cautions that free prizes do not last forever, 'which is why it's so essential that we get better at making new ones.'[22]

As in *Purple Cow*, Godin states that the reason why organizations do not create free prizes is down to fear. He states:

> They're scared.
> They're organized to resist change of any kind.
> They don't understand that soft innovation isn't risky, it's free and important.
> They don't realize how much their bosses want them to pursue soft innovations.

They've never been sold on doing it and they've never been taught how to do it well.[23]

If it ain't broke, don't fix it

If I had a penny for every time I heard about a library director that didn't believe in marketing because 'our patrons are happy ... we get very few complaints,' well, I'd have a lot of pennies ... but that's not the point. According to Tom Peters, Seth Godin, and many others, *not* getting complaints is a problem. Godin states: 'If the place where you work is successful at all, your company's biggest goal is probably to keep the satisfied customers happy.' Godin argues this is a problem because satisfied customers are 'unlikely to push you and your colleagues to stay ahead of the competition. One day, in fact, the competition will pass you and the satisfied customers will quietly leave.'[24]

It sounds scarily like the scenario where we wake up one day and our patrons are reading books and sipping cappuccino at the local Barnes & Noble while the library sits empty. How can we get our patrons to complain?

If the USPS can do it ...

Godin discusses how the USPS used a soft innovation by letting customers vote for which events would be commemorated with the millennium stamp. Azeez Jaffer came up with the idea and realized he would have to go through many layers of bureaucracy in order to make it happen. The deadline of the impending millennium helped him to move through the various levels of bureaucracy, and most importantly through the Citizens' Stamp Advisory Committee, which typically takes five to seven years to make a stamp happen. Jaffer also worked though the numbers – he found that this stamp would add $50 million to the bottom line.[25]

So how can you use Jaffer's idea? The Cambridge Public Library (CPL) is an example of a library that used a similar tactic to choose their mascot. They let the public vote, and they eventually chose Bamboo the Panda. It's unclear if Bamboo added $50 million to CPL's bottom line, but this marketing tactic helped to empower the community and showed them that their opinion mattered. (What pandas have to do with books is another story ...)

Notes

1. Seth Godin (2003) *Purple Cow – Transform Your Business by Being Remarkable*. New York: Penguin Group.
2. Seth Godin (2004) *Free Prize Inside: The Next Big Marketing Idea*. New York: Penguin Group.
3. Seth Godin (2003) *99 Cows*. New York: Do You Zoom.
4. Available at: *http://www.sethgodin.com/purple/99cows/moogle/* (accessed 31 July 2007).
5. Godin, *Purple Cow*, p. 16.
6. Ibid., p. 45.
7. Ibid., p. 49.
8. Ibid.
9. Ibid., p. 70.
10. Ibid., p. 67.
11. Jim Collins (2001) *Good to Great: Why Some Companies Make the Leap ... and Others Don't*. New York: HarperCollins, p. 1.
12. Godin, *Purple Cow*, p. 67.
13. Ibid., p. 77.

14. Ibid., p. 79.
15. Ibid., p. 92.
16. Ibid., p. 136.
17. Ibid.
18. Ibid.
19. Godin, *Free Prize Inside*, p. 238.
20. Ibid., p. 32.
21. Ibid., p. 5.
22. Ibid., p. 37.
23. Ibid., p. 41.
24. Ibid
25. Ibid., p. 116.

6

Finding the $$$

Introduction

This chapter assumes that you've done some planning and come up with a budget for your marketing initiatives. It also assumes that you believe you have the ability to get the program off the ground – congratulations on taking the first step. This chapter will explain how to 'sell' your ideas in order to get the resources needed to fund them.

Power

In *Free Prize Inside*, Seth Godin argues that organizations have small pockets of power within them. These pockets are made up of influential individuals who have opinions that carry much more weight than the average person's. He states 'you need to figure out who these influencers are, who they listen to and what they want.'[1] He offers several tactics for getting ideas accepted by those people. Some of these tactics include:

- ask questions;
- ask obligating questions;

- let them pee on your idea;
- people don't like to say 'no';
- dare them to improve your idea;
- acknowledge the status quo (and what's wrong with it);
- build a prototype;
- the gimme cap.[2]

Ask questions

Asking questions opens up a dialogue between yourself and your colleagues. You don't need to have the answers (and Godin asserts that it's better if you are perceived *not* to have the answers). The questions serve as a starting point.

Ask obligating questions

Godin states: 'People will put roadblocks in your way. They will object. They will explain why it can't be done.'[3] He suggests that answering their objections is not a good idea because if you spend all your time answering objections, sooner or later you will come across one that you can't. He explains there is a better way – to answer their questions with questions. For example:

> *Objection* : 'We will never be able to attract teenagers to come to the library.'
> *Question*: 'Why not?'

Godin suggests working backward until you find the actual problem – not just the symptoms. Additionally, Godin suggests two tactics to obligate the objector to help out. The first is to ask something like: 'If I can find a medium that teens will listen to, can you think of any other reason not to move ahead with our plan to market the library to teens?' This forces the objector to think through their objection and get to the heart of the problem … and it ensures that you are dealing with the actual problem and not a stalling tactic. The second part, Godin suggests, is to get them on your side.[4] He suggests asking: 'If I could persuade you that getting teenagers to use the library is really important, how would you do it?'

Let them pee on your idea

Godin states: 'Often those in positions to hurt (or help) your cause want to pee on your idea as a way of marking their territory. Let them.'[5] Godin explains that the minute someone changes your idea in a minor way, it becomes their idea, and you both win. He further states: 'Some champions go so far as to intentionally overlook details in their concepts to make it easier for someone in power to dramatically improve their idea. Why not?'[6]

People don't like to say 'no'

When you present your marketing plan, most likely no one will say 'no' to it. It's also unlikely they will say an enthusiastic 'Yes!!!! DO it!!' either. According to Godin, 'There are plenty of organizations where the usual response is to do nothing, or to stall, or to object, but not too strenuously.'[7] It's your job to prevail (refer back to Chapter 1 for reasons you need to market your library if necessary). Godin argues: 'If you can look someone in the eye and say "I'm going to make this happen unless you insist that I stop," more often than not you will get what you ask for.'[8]

Dare them to improve your idea

This tactic is about getting the people you work with on the same side of the fence you are on. Instead of focusing on, for example, the initial amount of extra work that may be involved, focus instead on how your marketing plan can help fix problems in their areas.

Godin believes this can be accomplished if two goals are kept in mind:

1. Encourage each person to make your idea better.
2. Get each person you meet with to start thinking of it as his or her idea.[9]

Godin believes that even timid people who despise change have big enough egos to help you brainstorm your marketing ideas, and they will be particularly interested if it helps solve problems in their area (i.e. not enough time or money budgeted for their initiatives).

Acknowledge the status quo

If your marketing plan is going to disrupt the status quo, be certain to be very clear how much trouble the existing situation is going to cost the library if it does not take action now. Refer to Chapter 1 for ideas.

Build a prototype

Is your library's website boring? Confusing? Difficult to find information on? It's very easy to build a prototype using various software programs (Photoshop, FrontPage, etc.). Show others what good library websites look like. Here are a few examples:

- *http://www.nypl.org/*
- *http://tamworthlibrary.org/*
- *http://www.spl.org/*

The gimme cap

Godin believes that once ideas start spreading though an organization, there will only be two teams: those that are for you, and those that are against you. He suggests giving out a visible sign, such as a cap or tee shirt, to let others share your vision – and that the marketing initiative is going to happen, is likely to succeed, and is worth doing.[10] The following exercise will to help put your marketing ideas in motion.

Exercise 6.1   Create a prototype

Put together a brochure for an upcoming program. Design a new library logo. Create a tee shirt for your summer reading program. Your marketing prototypes make your idea concrete and reinforce the thought that this plan will go forward.

Notes

1. Seth Godin (2004) *Free Prize Inside: The Next Big Marketing Idea*. New York: Penguin Group, p. 85.
2. Ibid., pp. 87–99.
3. Ibid., p. 87.
4. Ibid.
5. Ibid., p. 88.
6. Ibid., p. 90.
7. Ibid.
8. Ibid.
9. Ibid., p. 94.
10. Ibid.

Market research

Introduction

Of critical importance in putting together a marketing plan is to conduct market research. After all, if you don't have a way to figure out who is using your library, how do you know you are accomplishing the library's mission? Yet most libraries don't do any kind of research to ensure that they are achieving their goals. Libraries that do claim to research their constituencies usually depend on circulation stats or informal head counts. Most libraries I've consulted with, as well as my library school students, report that they see changes in demographics of their town (such as cultural shifts) but this is not reflected in the people they see in their libraries. This chapter will discuss how to go about conducting a small-scale research project and assumes no prior market research background. If you have some background research experience, you might want to skim the chapter and see if you need to brush up on any particular topics. If you need to conduct a more extensive research project, please refer to the additional resources at the end of the chapter.

Definition of market research

According to the American Marketing Association, market research is defined as:

> The function that links the consumer, customer, and public to the marketer through information – used to identify and define marketing opportunities and problems; generate, refine, and evaluate marketing actions; monitor marketing performance; and improve understanding of marketing as a process. Marketing research specifies the information required to address these issues, designs the method for collecting information, manages and implements the data collection process, analyzes the results, and communicates the findings and their implications.[1]

Clearly market research is a critical component of a library's marketing plan. This chapter will break down the components of market research and discuss how you can go about putting together a plan for your library.

Importance of conducting market research

According to Barry McLeish, without conducting market research, a nonprofit organization cannot accurately determine which marketing strategies work, which causes should be implemented, and which products currently are appropriate for the target markets. He also states that research and analysis produces a better understanding of the market opportunities, the potential effectiveness of the promotional dollars being spent, and the obstacles to be overcome.[2]

Additionally, market research helps organizations stay in touch with customers' changing attitudes. It assists libraries in better understanding opportunities. Also, it can help determine the feasibility of a particular marketing strategy. This is a critical point, as it can save the library time and money in the early stages if, for example, the library program lacks interest in the early stages of testing.

Market research also aids in developing marketing mixes to match the needs of patrons and improves the library's ability to make decisions regarding which products, services, and programs to offer.

The market research process

As indicated in the definition above, there are several processes involved in the market research process. We will break the process down into five steps: defining the research problem, designing the project, collecting data, interpreting the results, and reporting the findings.

Defining the research problem

The first step in the market research process is to define the research problem or issue. This is the most important step in any marketing plan, because if the library spends hundreds or thousands of dollars doing market research but has not correctly identified the problem, those dollars are wasted. Examples of library market issues may include researching why particular groups do not come to the library or if there is a need for a particular library program. Once the marketing problem or issue is defined, objectives for the market research need to be decided upon. A good question to ask is, what information is needed to help solve the problem? Are you trying to increase the number of 25–30 year olds that use the library? Are you trying to attract a particular ethnic group? If so, you would need to find out the number of 25–30 year olds that are currently using the library and compare it with the demographic information, for example, for your city or town if you are marketing a public library.

Designing the research project

The next step is to design the research project. The research design is the overall plan for obtaining the information needed to address the marketing problem or issue.

The person conducting the research will form what is known as a hypothesis, an informed guess or assumption about a certain problem or set of circumstances. There are three broad categories of research design: exploratory, descriptive, and causal.

Exploratory research tends to be the first step in a larger research process. If you don't know the scope of the research problem, exploratory research may help to focus and guide your future research. For example, you might set time aside to observe who is currently using your library as a first step in determining who is not and why. The 'who is not using your library and why' could be considered to be *descriptive* research. Descriptive research looks at how certain variables affect each other, such as user attitudes, intentions, and behaviors. Most likely, you will be conducting descriptive research, so we will focus on this particular type of research design in this chapter. *Causal* research involves looking at what variable causes another to happen by controlling various factors and looking at the effects of manipulating the variables. This type of research design is often referred to as experimental research design.

Collecting the data

There are two basic types of information that are used in research designs: secondary and primary data. Secondary data is information that has already been collected. Examples include government census data, industry publications and databases, or any internal information that the library collects regarding circulation statistics, seasonal library usage, etc. Primary data is data that is collected directly from respondents. Examples include any study the library has done, for example to look at perceptions of customer service in the library.

In order to collect the data, a few decisions need to be made. The first is regarding the scope of your marketing research plan. It is usually impossible to get results from an entire population, for example getting a response from everyone in a particular town that a public library is located in. Therefore a sample of the population is used. In order for the results of your market research to have any credibility whatsoever, you will need to ensure that that sample is representative of the population as a whole. This generally means that if you know that you have 7,000 pink people, 3,000 purple people and 5,000 green people, your sample will have representative proportions of each type of person. If you do a survey and you only have green people responding, that will skew your results to the opinions, attitudes, preferences, etc. of only green people (which is fine if you are only interested in green people, but if you want the others included, you need to find ways to reach them in your research process). There are three main types of sampling, each with inherent pros and cons: probability or random, stratified, and nonprobability. With probability sampling, each element has a known chance of being included. This is also commonly referred to as random sampling. Stratified sampling is when the study population is divided into like groups (such as male/female) and then probability sampling is used. With nonprobability sampling, each element's likelihood of study is unknown. Using quotas is a type of nonprobability sampling. Generally probability sampling is considered to be a more 'scientific' approach and has better results. Nonprobability sampling tends to be less costly in terms of time and money. Your particular research problem/issue, as well as time and budget constraints, will generally dictate which type of sampling you will use.

There are four main ways to collect data and each also has its relative advantages and disadvantages. These methods include mail, telephone, online, and in-person surveys.

Mail

Two main issues come into play when using a mail survey. The first is the response rate. Unsolicited mail surveys typically have a very low response rate. Generally if one percent of people you send out your survey to respond to it, you're doing very well. Therefore marketers have come up with several ways to try to improve the rate of response from their mail surveys. Generally, they involve some sort of incentive. Including a dollar bill to thank the person for their time sometimes works by 'obligating' the person to do the survey. Other marketers state in the survey that their name will be included in a draw for a valued prize, for example an iPod, a coupon for a local restaurant, an all-expenses-paid trip to Tahiti, etc. Other incentives include a note from a celebrity or well known figurehead in the area, explaining the importance of the cause and why it is critical for the respondent to return the survey. Well-designed mail surveys with good response rates can be of lower cost per respondent than in-person or telephone surveys. The other issue that affects response rates with mail surveys has to do with the list of respondents that is used. Typically many businesses will sell lists of people's names and addresses in a particular area that can be broken down by zip code, interests, income, or other demographics ... but, of course, the list is only as good as the organization selling it to you makes it. If the list-selling organization does not update the database very often, you could wind up with a large number of addresses and names of people that are not living there anymore – and then you will have to deal with the frustrating flood of 'return to sender' envelopes in your mailbox rather than returned surveys with valuable information.

Other negatives with mail surveys include lack of flexibility – your questionnaire must be short with questions that are easy to answer, and those questions cannot be changed once the survey is mailed out. On the positive side, researcher bias can be eliminated, and other items, such as coupons and other information such as calendars and program announcements, can be included.

Telephone

OK, I can see you rolling your eyes at the thought of conducting a telephone survey. Everyone loves to have their dinner interrupted by a telemarketer, even if their call is for a higher purpose such as making the library a better place for them, right? Most people *love* to run to the phone, only to find out that it's not that job offer that they've been waiting for, but *you* on the phone doing market research for your library, right? All right, you know the negatives involved with this type of data collection. I'm not trying to convince you that you need to do it. I'm going to point out a few of the reasons that *other* people use this method, then I'll quickly move on to the last two types of data collection. I promise.

Telephone interviews can be less expensive than in-person interviews. Unlike mail and online surveys, the research can account for tone and can ask probing questions so there is more flexibility. Flexibility, though, opens the door for researcher bias. And, of course, you probably already know about caller ID and various other technological devices (such as the 'Gotta Go' call waiting imitator discussed in Chapter 4), do-not-call lists, and the like, that may make getting a representative sample difficult, at best. OK, done. Let's move on.

Online

Online surveys are generally considered to be the most economical, given a good response rate. The pitfalls are similar to mail surveys, so good e-mail address lists and incentives can improve that response rate. E-mail surveys also have similar lack of flexibility, but they have the additional issues of needing to be easy for online users to receive and return. Short, dichotomous (two options such as yes/no) and multiple choice options tend to work best in online surveys. Many library users swear by surveymonkey.com, which allows users to develop and collect surveys with prices that range from free to $200 a year. Zoomerang.com also offers similar products and services.

Challenges with online surveys include the limitation of responses to people who know how to use computers, and that e-mail addresses may not include a representative sample for some purposes.

In-person interviews

In-person surveys will likely reveal the greatest depth of information for your marketing dollar – assuming that is what you need for your research project. With in-person interviews, the person conducting the interview has a host of nonverbal feedback that can be used, they can ask probing questions and they can respond to questions that the respondent may have. But as you may have guessed, this type of research tends to be the most expensive. Generally the interviews take place at home, but shopping mall intercepts have become more popular (and solves the problem of people not being home at the time of the interview). One of the main problems with in-person interviews, other than the cost, is researcher bias. Generally the greater the flexibility with the question and responses, the greater the possibility for researcher bias.

Focus groups are another type of in-person interview. Generally people in the target market group are invited to come into the library to discuss the market research problem/issue. Most focus groups involve some sort of incentive, usually cash or some type of refreshment (usually pizza, particularly in academic libraries – a strong incentive for college students!). Because these interviews are conducted in groups, it can be cost-effective, even for small libraries.

The research instrument

The design of the research instrument is also critical to the success of the marketing research process. Generally a questionnaire is used. The instrument used should be reliable and valid, that is, the questionnaire should yield similar results when it is used over and over again and measure what it sets out to measure. The easiest way to obtain a reliable and valid questionnaire is to find one that another library has used and had good results with, even if it means paying a small fee. Using another library's survey instrument could be a problem if you are looking at a different variable, but I thought I'd throw the idea out there … why reinvent the wheel if you don't have to?

If you do need to create your own instrument, the questions you will use will fall into one of two categories: structured and non-structured. *Structured* questions consist of closed-ended questions, for example multiple choice or dichotomous questions. They also can include questions with a scale; for example, 'on a scale of 1 to 7 rate how you feel about the library's new purple polka dot color scheme' with 1 being 'absolutely love' and 7 being 'makes me want to retch.' *Unstructured* questions have open-ended answers, so respondents can choose their own words and responses. Obviously, it is much easier to record and perform an analysis on a large number of responses using structured questions. However, if depth of information is needed, or just a small number of responses are to be analyzed, unstructured questions may be the better choice.

Interpreting the results

The way the results are interpreted will depend on the research design. In most cases, if you are conducting descriptive research with a large number of responses, some type of statistical interpretation will shed light on the results. Software programs such as Minitab and SPSS can help to determine how widely the responses vary, how the responses are distributed, which hypotheses are supported or rejected, or if construction errors have invalidated the survey's results.

Reporting the findings

The last step in the research process is to report your results. This will depend again on the research design and your process. If you are reporting the results of your marketing research plan to your director of board of trustees, then you may need to summarize the results into a formal written document. First take an objective look at your findings and own up to any possible problems in the research process. Then summarize the results in a clear, simple format, discuss what the findings mean for the library, and offer any relevant suggestions based on your results. If you found problems with the research design, construction, or implantation of your survey, you might want to state that the study should be repeated at a given time interval to help validate the results.

Additional resources

Krueger, Richard A. and Casey, Mary Anne (2000) *Focus Groups: A Practical Guide for Applied Research*, 3rd edn. Thousand Oaks, CA: Sage.

McQarrie, Edward (2005) *The Market Research Toolbox: A Concise Guide for Beginners*, 2nd edn. Thousand Oaks, CA: Sage.

SPSS Statistical Software: *http://www.spss.com*.

Notes

1. See: *http://www.marketingpower.com/content4620.php* (accessed 17 July 2007).
2. Barry McLeish (1995) *Successful Marketing Strategies for Nonprofit Organizations*. New York: John Wiley & Sons.

8

Branding

Introduction

As marketplace competition heightens and consumers become more savvy and sophisticated, organizations must work harder than ever to secure and retain their customers. One of the most effective ways organizations have found to achieve this goal is to focus on branding their services. For example:

- *Just do it*
- *Have it your way*
- *Be all that you can be*

What do these have in common? They create an expectation and a promise. It's called branding.

What is a brand?

Although the tendency is to associate the word 'brand' with a logo or slogan, branding is much more than that. A brand encapsulates everything that should come to mind when one thinks of a specific organization, product, or service. According to Allen Adamson:

A brand is something that lives in your head. It is a promise that links a product or service to a consumer. Whether words, images, or emotions, or any combination of the three, brands are mental associations that get stirred up when you think or hear about a particular car or camera, watch, pair of jeans, bank, beverage, TV network, organization, celebrity, or even country.[1]

The strongest brands work hard to build clear, positive images in consumers' minds.

Scott Bedbury, the man responsible for helping to brand Nike and Starbucks, describes brands as follows:

A great brand taps into emotions ... Emotions drive most, if not all, of our decisions. A brand reaches out with a powerful connecting experience. It's an emotional connecting point that transcends the product ... A great brand is a story that's never completely told. A brand is a metaphorical story that's evolving all the time ... Stories create the emotional context people need to locate themselves in a larger experience.[2]

The process of branding an organization is a long and complex one. In order for branding to occur, much thought and energy must go into what exactly will live behind the brand itself. The entire identity of the organization must be built and managed so as to be in tune with the brand that is shown to the customer. A key point to keep in mind is that while the process of creating the brand is quite complicated, the end result must be simple – the associations that the organization wants the consumer to make must be easy and intuitive, otherwise the brand will not be accepted.[3]

Beyond building the brand itself, marketers have several related aspects to keep in mind. Organizations must build strong advertising campaigns in order to promote their brand. They can also turn to celebrity endorsements and creating emotional or symbolic relationships with their target market in order to make their brand a strong, successful one. With the advent of the Internet and the fact that creating a brand has become more the norm than the exception to the rule, organizations must work very hard to create a distinct image for themselves.

History

Branding has been around since goods were first traded in ancient times. Craftsmen's marks date back to 3000 BC in India. Trademarks have also been found on Greek and Roman lamps, Chinese porcelain, and Egyptian paintings. In 1266, English law required bakers to put their mark on every loaf of bread so that, in case of a weight or price discrepancy, customers could identify the guilty party. The early American colonies saw branding with homeopathic medicines peddled from carts and pharmacies. The first US trademark law was enacted in 1870, requiring all registrants to send a copy of their mark and a description of their product with $25 to the Patent Office. One of the first trademarks to be registered was the Devil, registered to Underwood & Company of Boston, Massachusetts.[4]

Over the centuries, the concept of branding has grown to become more than just a distinguishing mark. In the US specifically, branded products began to take on a different type of significance after the Civil War. With improvements in transportation, production processes, and packaging, along with increased industrialization, the market was geared for the creation of nationally marketed branded products.[5] Consumers began to trust the nationally branded products as they knew what to expect in terms of reliability and quality.

In subsequent years, mass marketed brands began to take over from the traditional reliance on locally made products. As these mass marketed brands gained wider acceptance, the marketing techniques used to sell them became more complex and specialized. The years 1914–29 saw the rise of design experts employed to create logos and advertising. During this time, the process of branding was relatively simple. With little competition, the brand's message had a higher chance of reaching the target market. With such little competition for consumers' attention, an organization could safely assume that their brand would create a successful image in consumers' minds. [6]

A sharp decline took place during the Second World War, as all resources were directed toward the war. The 1950s and beyond saw an explosion of brands that continues today as a result of the growing middle class. Also, over the past 30 years, what it means to brand a particular product or service has drastically changed. The past few decades have seen the amount of branded products and services available on the market skyrocket, making the task of creating a distinguishable brand much more difficult. Today, almost everything is branded – products as mundane as water or as high-profile as a famous person all have a brand stamp on them. With an increased amount of communication channels, particularly the Internet, organizations have the ability to display their brand almost anywhere.[7] In fact, you can put your pooch to work with 'dog-vertising' (banners belted onto the side of your beagle) or have college kids help fund their tuition with 'head-vertising' – a logo stenciled onto your freshman's forehead.[8]

Some experts say that branding reached its peak in 1996 when McDonald's and Disney agreed to cross promote each other's brands.[9]

Creating a brand

How does an organization go about creating a brand which will lead to brand awareness and ultimately brand loyalty? First, they must create a unique character or personality, a core principle that will set their reputation. They must be narrow enough in their uniqueness where they can have the largest impact. Second, they must build a relationship with their target market. Market research must be done to figure out who is in the target market and how they can be reached effectively. Third, they must create a visual image. This image must be well thought out and done correctly so that it will elicit an emotional response when seen. This image, symbol, or logo must remain consistent in all the organization's advertising and publicity. The logo itself will not create loyalty. The image should portray the most positive attributes associated with the service or product.[10]

The cost of branding can be quite high, but the organization should consider the benefits as well. These include easier selling and tracking of orders, protecting the brand legally though the use of trademarks, attracting loyalty, and helping organizations to segment their market and build an organizational image. Brands help distinguish one product from another and create a competitive advantage. Organizations that have brand awareness have a stronger likelihood of sustaining their business and this can lead to growth in new products and services.[11]

Branding your library

In an age where nearly everything is branded, creating a brand name for the library is a good way of keeping the library current. Building a brand for the library helps to create a clear picture of what the library is and what it stands for in the eyes of the patrons. The library should already have a mission or vision statement (as discussed in Chapter 2). According to Beth Dempsey, 'if [libraries] are brand driven, the mission statement puts into words how the brand ... will be delivered. It makes ... a "brand promise" to the customer.'[12] A brand is attached to a product or service which consumers tend to grow to know and trust. By creating a brand for the library, patrons can come to depend on the library to provide certain products and services.

Libraries are in a prime space to brand their services. True, libraries face many challenges in branding intangible services like reference, instruction, and the use of and access to databases. They also face financial challenges (as well as a loss of identity, as on the Web where open access information has become confused with licensed databases), but the opportunity to present a positive experience to their customer base should not be ignored.

Charles Fisher's article *The Library's Living Brand* introduces the marketing principle of branding and attempts to apply it to libraries in an effort to increase public awareness of the importance of library services and to draw users away from what he considers other, less valuable resources, like Amazon and Google.[13] Fisher suggests that libraries should attempt to become living brands, an idea drawn from an article he references by Neeli and Venkat Bendapudi titled 'Creating the living brand' in the *Harvard Business Review*. Fisher suggests that since library staff are the resource that the library would be attempting to brand, then using three of the living brand's principles – talent, community, and security/esteem/justice – to hone library staff and increase development is the key to branding libraries and attracting and maintaining patrons.[14]

Fisher offers simple options for each of the three principles which libraries could implement without radically changing any of their current management approaches but which would, if successfully implemented, contribute to an overall improvement in staff attitude, aptitude, and performance. For contributing to and developing the talent principle, Fisher suggests creating a formal mentor program, improving customer service, and establishing continuing education. For building a sense of community, Fisher suggests focusing on the library in terms of space, and again improving customer service. For the final principle, Fisher explores several ways to encourage job security, and he suggests creating a mechanism for feedback from both patrons to library staff and among library staff themselves. Fisher's conclusion encourages bringing all three principles together to ensure the library is investing in itself to better serve patrons, in the hopes that, in his example, a patron might in one instance choose the library over Google.[15]

It is important to realize that a brand is more than a logo – it is a way of life. For any organization, its brand should be 'stamped' on every aspect, from its products and services to its look and feel. For a library, where the goal is not to sell a product or service, the library's brand should encapsulate what the library feels its value to the community is. More importantly, according to Beth Dempsey, 'the library's brand is the space that you've captured in the minds of the customers – it's all the things that come to mind, all the expectations they have, when they hear the word *library*.'[16]

Dempsey, like many others, argues that the library has much to learn from corporate America, citing Borders, Target, and Starbucks as key examples. For each, the 'brand is more than the logo – it is the whole experience associated with the company.' Customers know what to expect when entering these stores, and in the case of Target and Starbucks, they can easily spot one of their products when away from the store. If the library is going to successfully compete with places like Borders, Barnes & Noble, and other bookstores, it also needs to create a consistent, professional feeling brand that forms a clear identity and defines the library's value in the community.

One of the most important pieces of advice that Dempsey offers is the need to be consistent, not only in the 'look' itself, but how it is applied. The library must plan how to implement its brand and make sure that every aspect of service reflects this brand. Dempsey also cautions against changing the library's brand once it is laid down – yes, it can be tweaked, but a full change to the brand can be offputting for the library's patrons. A consistent brand will allow patrons to know what to expect.[17]

Exercise 8.1   Branding alphabet

Go to http://www.medialit.org/reading_room/article637 .html. *How many brands in the letters do you recognize?*

Exercise 8.2   Branding your library

Think about ways you can brand your library. What images would you use? How would you ensure consistency with your library brand's words and images?

Notes

1. Allen Adamson (2006) *BrandSimple: How the Best Brands Keep It Simple and Succeed*. New York: Palgrave Macmillan.
2. Scott Bedbury, as quoted in Tom Peters (1999) *The Brand You 50*. New York: Alfred Knopf, p. 26.
3. Adamson, *BrandSimple*.
4. 'Branding through the ages,' *Telephony*, 1996, 231 (6): 32.
5. Adamson, *BrandSimple*.
6. Ibid.
7. Kevin Lane Keller (2003) *Strategic Brand Management: Building, Measuring, and Managing Brand Equity*, 2nd edn. Englewood Cliffs, NJ: Prentice Hall.
8. Linda Kaplan-Thaler and Robin Koval (2003) *Bang! Getting Your Message Heard in a Noisy World*. New York: Currency Books, p. 3.
9. 'Branding through the ages,' p. 32.
10. Philip Kotler (2000) *Marketing Management*, 10th edn. Englewood Cliffs, NJ: Prentice Hall, pp. 404–17.
11. Ibid.
12. Beth Dempsey (2004) 'Target your brand: build an identity that works in the age of the superstore,' *Library Journal*, 129 (13): 32–5.
13. See: *http://www.aallnet.org/products/pub_sp0612/pub_sp0612_brand.pdf*.
14. Neeli Bendapudi and Venkat Bendapudi (2005) 'Creating the living brand,' *Harvard Business Review*, 1 May.
15. Ibid.
16. Ibid.
17. Dempsey, 'Target your brand.'

9

Buzz

Introduction

Buzz marketing is an attempt to create a trend or acceptance of a product through word-of-mouth communications. It is a growing field of research as very little was known about it until around the year 2000. Here are some interesting statistics that get at the importance of this relatively new marketing tactic:

- Sixty-five percent of customers that bought a palm organizer reported that they had heard about it from another person.

- Friends and relatives are the #1 source for information about places to visit or about flights, hotels, or rental cars, according to the Travel Industry Association.

- Fifty-three percent of moviegoers rely to some extent on a recommendation from someone they know. No matter how much money Hollywood pours into advertising, people frequently consult with each other about what movie to see.[1]

Clearly, we rely heavily on communications with other people when making decisions.

Buzz defined

What is buzz? In his book *The Power of Cult Branding*, Emmanuel Rosen defines 'buzz' as 'all the word of mouth about a brand. It's the aggregate of all person-to-person communication about a particular product, service, or company at any point in time.'[2] Essentially, Rosen's broad definition focuses on comments that are exchanged between people about products and services.

The buzz on buzz

As stated in various chapters throughout this book, old marketing strategies, particularly advertising, are becoming less effective. The cause is said to be twofold: first, technology is becoming so advanced that traditional advertising such as TV advertising is being suppressed by potential customers that just don't want to listen. Secondly, personal communications have increased to the point where you are more likely to buy or use a product that has been recommended via word of mouth. Several new rules are presented by Steve Brooks in his article 'How to build buzzzzzz.'[3]

The first new rule involves checking the Internet for any buzz involving the product or service to see what consumers are saying. Brooks highlights blogs in particular here, and urges businesses to create their own blogs to reach their potential consumers through a medium that they are more likely to read.

The second new rule concerns what Brooks calls 'connectors,' also cited in Malcolm Gladwell's book *The Tipping Point*.[4] The connectors are those people that have a higher degree of influence than the rest of the public. By influencing the connectors to promote the product or service, they will in turn tell friends and acquaintances, thereby creating added demand for the product or service. This rule stresses primarily verbal communication, including listening to customers about what they want.

Rule three discusses surprising customers (similar to *Made to Stick* by Chip and Dan Heath, discussed in Chapter 3). Surprising customers could involve distributing a new product in an interesting way, or offering a unique service. The fourth rule is to 'spread a virus,' similar to both Gladwell's 'sneezers'[5] and Seth Godin's 'ideavirus.'[6] This involves the use of viral advertising (word-of-mouth advertising taken to the Web). Viral advertising involves sending special announcements electronically and urging them to be passed onto your friends. The advantage of this method is exponential advertising, but it also carries the disadvantage of having a lack of control. Brooks's final rule promotes the use of commercial text messages. The main advantage is the speed with which the message can get to the right person, but it can also be expensive. Brooks frames this as the technological equivalent of print advertising and worth the price.[7]

Brooks's 'rules' are particularly well suited to public libraries. Many libraries have already instituted some of his strategies. For example, both public and private libraries have begun to use blogs as a way of telling their patrons about what is happening at the library in any given week or month. In addition, some people blog about their library experiences. This is particularly relevant at colleges and universities. At Trinity College in Hartford, Connecticut (see Chapter 2) many students posted blogs protesting a new policy of signing in at the library front desk. Blogs can be used to introduce staff members to patrons and to display librarians' favorite books. Displaying favorite books is a way to encourage patrons to develop a dialog with staff members about their research or literary interests. One of the most common reasons people in libraries do not ask for help is that they see the image of the librarian as an intimidating one – a blog could open up the communication channel.

The second rule is particularly useful to public libraries. Allen Smith, Professor of Reference Services at Simmons College's Graduate School of Library and Information Sciences, imparts the following wisdom to all his students: 'If you are a public librarian, get out in the community and make sure everyone important in town, from firefighters to the selectmen, know who you are.' While Brooks has replaced the important people with the term 'connectors,' the sentiment is similar. First and foremost, in a budget situation, it is important for town officials to realize the importance of the library. The public librarian acts as the face of the library and is therefore primarily responsible for connecting with influential people in town who can help secure necessary funds. If an ordinary townsperson sees that the town officials care about the library, they will be more likely to use it, or at the very least support it. Therefore, according to Brooks's example, influencing the trendsetters will likely increase exposure exponentially.

Rule three is essentially innovation rewarded. It is essential for libraries, like every other organization, to remain innovative. The image of a library as a sacred place filled with dusty volumes and little old ladies 'shushing' people is prevalent. By introducing new innovations and successfully spreading the word, the library can surprise its customers. For example, a library can introduce reduced fines depending on how many books you take out at once. It could also offer weekly lists by e-mail of new books that an individual might like, similar to Amazon.com.

Nevertheless, surprising customers with new and interesting services can make them come back, even just to see if something else new is happening. The goal is to make the library appear as a motion filled, happening place instead of a stagnant repository.

Brooks's fourth rule has many disadvantages in the commercial world largely because it gets out of control and often money is involved. However, sending e-mails to patrons and urging them to pass on the information would be ideal for libraries. In fact, it is surprising that more libraries do not have an e-mail list where patrons can sign up for various promotions and for programming events to be sent to them. One way this rule has been applied in the commercial world is the Tide Cold Water promotion. In the promotion, people could calculate how much energy they were saving and then could send it onto their friends to amaze them into trying the product. A similar promotion has been attempted at the Maine State Library which allows patrons to see how much they are saving by using the library (*http://www.maine.gov/msl/services/calculator.htm*). What is missing with this calculator is the ability to send along the information to friends. Regardless, having the ability to e-mail patrons via an e-mail signup list could add additional patrons or simply keep loyal patrons informed.

The fifth rule may be the least applicable to libraries because the events and promotions that happen in the library are not urgent enough to warrant text messages or spending money for the service. As Allen Smith says: 'There are no emergencies in the library world.' While flood, fire, and murder could all happen in the library, they are rare, and do not justify the cost of using text messaging. However, the library could use text messaging for an instant reference service, or even to answer simple questions about the library or its programs.

The largest part of Brooks's article is his overarching theme of communication. He realizes both that communication is an important part of marketing and that current communication tools such as print, telephone, and television are rapidly being surpassed by more technologically advanced tools such as the Web, blogs, text messaging, and others. These tools are making it easier to share personal opinions about services as well as placing a higher value on personal opinion than ever before. Therefore libraries, like any other service, must step forward to make sure that the patron's personal opinion and image of the library is a positive one in order to both obtain and keep new patrons that have not used the library before.

Buzz or stealth marketing?

Related to 'buzz' is the concept of 'stealth marketing.' In a recent article by Andrew and Jack Kaikati, the authors discuss stealth marketing and the three factors that have made it popular in recent years. First, the advertising industry in general has garnered criticism for not delivering messages to target audiences. In many situations, the traditional 30-second television commercial has not been effective. Second, with the increase in media outlets, audiences have become fragmented, therefore potential customers are harder to reach. Third, personal video recorders and digital video have made it possible for viewers to skip advertising entirely.[8]

The article also describes the various types of stealth marketing that have been used by the industry. The six popular techniques are:

- viral marketing, which is stealth marketing via a digital platform like the Internet;

- brand pushers, which is placing actors in public places to casually promote the product or service;

- celebrity marketing;

- bait and tease, which is creating covert campaigns for products;

- marketing in video games; and

- marketing in pop and rap music.

The authors discuss the strengths and weaknesses of stealth marketing. For example, this type of marketing is relatively inexpensive when compared to traditional advertising. However, marketers do not have as much control over the message as they would in a traditional advertisement. Additionally, there are ethical questions and implications surrounding this type of promotion, such as:

- Is it unethical to deceive people by hiring actors to plug a product in public?

- Is the use of stealth marketing diminishing music as an art form?

- Does this type of marketing cheapen the idea of truth in advertising?[9]

Aside from the ethical questions, this type of marketing strategy may be useful to librarians. Whether the librarian works in a public, academic, or special library, librarians need to be able to market their institutions to their patrons. If patrons do not know about the services offered by the library, and recognize value in those services, they will not use the library. Therefore, librarians need to be aware of the various ways to publicize these services. Because libraries do not usually have a large marketing budget, knowledge of nontraditional strategies like stealth marketing becomes even more important.

It is very likely that librarians may not be able to use many of the strategies in the Kaikatis' article. Libraries will probably not be able to get Paris Hilton to carry around the most popular books from their collection during a night out. They will also have trouble getting the makers of *Grand Theft Auto* to include a reference desk in their newest game. And they will probably not convince Jay-Z that he should rap about the fantastic free databases that the library offers. However, libraries could learn from the information on word-of-mouth marketing and creating buzz. For instance, even though libraries cannot usually afford to pay actors to visit public places and promote services, they could convert this idea into manageable and affordable marketing. For instance, a public library could have its librarians attend town meetings and events. The librarians could casually talk about the library at these events. In this way, they are creating word-of-mouth publicity for the library.

Libraries could also use the article's example of Hotmail employing viral marketing. Every e-mail sent by a Hotmail account tells the recipient that he or she can start his or her own free Hotmail account. Perhaps an academic library could partner with the school's e-mail server to put messages about the library on the bottom of each e-mail sent by the system. An idea like this may be too commercial for the library, but it should consider new and inventive methods for marketing their services. More innovative ideas are discussed in Chapter 4.

Many myths surround the idea of buzz. Renée Dye's article 'The buzz on buzz' discusses basic 'buzz' principles that she has discovered through her research into the marketing practices of 50 companies. The common perception about buzz is that it is 'sheer luck' but her research shows that this 'phenomenon ... dubbed "explosive self-generating demand," is hardly a random force of nature.'[10]

Dye's research explores an organization's ability to predict the spread of buzz through analyzing how 'different groups of customers interact and influence each other.[11] The article describes the basic principles behind how buzz works by diffusing five myths about buzz. The first myth is that 'only outrageous or edgy products are buzz-worth.' Dye uses a chart which shows how much of the economy is affected by buzz, and which industries are affected the most. She attributes the role of buzz to the growth of technology and the ability of consumers to share their thoughts/feelings about a particular product. The article provides two criteria to determine if a product is buzz-worthy: if it is unique or if it is highly visible.

'Buzz just happens' is the second myth discussed in the article. Dye describes five marketing strategies – seed the vanguard, ration supply, exploit icons to beget buzz, tap the power of lists, and nurture grass roots. She states that any sequence and combination of these strategies can affect a product's buzz factor. The third myth is 'the best buzz-starts are your customers.' Here Dye provides examples such as Tommy Hilfiger to illustrate how countercultures can impact buzz. She also describes how managers can find these unexpected 'vanguards' – a group with the ability to influence public opinion – by collecting marketing data on how consumers influence one another about a product.

Dye states 'To profit from buzz, you must act first and fast' as her fourth myth. Dye dispels this myth by showing ways for 'copycats' to identify trends and the ways that they can use already established buzz to their advantage. The final myth that 'the media and advertising are needed to create buzz' is dispelled as Dye reveals that buzz is born through 'consumer-to-consumer communications.' The ultimate goal is to incite customers to talk about the product so that it is noticed by others, rather than bombarding them with advertising.[12]

Dye's myths relate to libraries in the following ways.

- *No. 1: Only outrageous or edgy products are buzz-worthy.* Dye discusses how buzz spreads by illustrating how Merck used a two-pronged approach to create buzz. First it used key figures to test and promote their product. Libraries, as discussed above, can use highly visible staff members in the community to promote certain library services. The second part of Merck's approach involved making the product visible. Libraries should also promote their programming in this way, as the more visible the services are, the more buzz will be created. Additionally, buzz can be created though forums. Libraries should use wikis and blogs in which patrons can discuss library services in order to make these services more visible. Dye also discusses how to assess 'buzz-worthiness' – one way is to show how a particular product or service is unique. Libraries can communicate that their services are 'free,' whereas most other organizations that offer similar products or services charge something to the user.

- *No. 2: Buzz just happens.* In discussing how buzz is created though the different elements of the marketing strategy, Dye stresses the importance of 'seeding the vanguard.' The vanguards shape public opinion, so libraries could seek out key members of the community who will tell their peers about the services at the library. For example, if the library offered services that teens became excited about, these teens are more likely to get other teens into the library than a poster or flyer. This type of buzz worked for the Plaistow Public Library when it created a mini-golf course on the library property. Teens enjoyed playing the games and told their friends, creating buzz for the library. The library was able to attract a hard-to-reach age group. Additionally, Dye discusses 'rationing supply' – the idea that people want what they can't have. One way the library can use this idea is through using signup sheets for certain programs. Patrons may wonder what makes this event so special that only a certain number of people can attend? Organizations have also used this theory through their websites. Certain portions of their sites require customers to register (through inputting their name, e-mail address, etc.). Libraries could set up their websites this way as well, with certain products or services (audio downloads, special programs) that require the user to register. Dye also discusses 'Tapping the power of lists' in order to create a road sign for customers. Libraries can also uses list services such as summer reading lists, 100 most popular books at the library, 100 most banned books, etc., as this will create a higher demand for the titles.

- *No. 3: The best buzz starters are your best customers.* Dye gets at the importance of collecting marketing data not only on what individuals think about a particular product, but also on how customers influence one another about the product. If this idea holds true, then potential and new library users would create more buzz than existing library users. Libraries could encourage new users to share their experiences with potential users.

- *No. 4: To profit from buzz, you must act first and fast.* Dye states 'Trendsetting companies may generate buzz, but copycat firms can also reap tremendous benefits.' Services such as book groups have become very popular at the library, therefore most libraries can easily implement this idea. Dye also stresses the importance of keeping on top of trends. Librarians should be aware of current events and pop culture. *Library Trends* is a journal that helps librarians do just that. Staying on top of trends will allow them to anticipate the needs and wants of patrons, in addition to identifying new services that would draw in potential users. The library can establish wikis and blogs for creating virtual focus groups on what patrons are thinking. Refer to Chapter 4 for more information on trends.

- *No. 5: Media and advertising are needed to create buzz.* The importance of 'consumer-to-consumer communications – be they verbal, visual, or digital' is stressed. Once again, libraries can facilitate consumer-to-consumer communications though the use of wikis and blogs. Dye also states how too much publicity can work against a product.

WOM

In his article, 'What's all the buzz about? Everyday communication and the relational basis of word-of-mouth and buzz marketing practices,' Walter Carl presents findings from a study on the impact of relationships on word-of-mouth (WOM) and 'buzz' marketing. Buzz marketing is an *institutional* form of WOM, where the topic of communication is part of an institutional marketing campaign. *Everyday* WOM, on the other hand, is informal communication in which participants are assumed or perceived to be freely sharing personal thoughts and opinions.[13]

Following a literature review of research into the role relational communication plays in marketing, Carl identifies a gap in the research into the role which everyday communication and relationships play in regard to buzz marketing 'agents.' Agents frequently are volunteers who choose to participate in a buzz marketing campaign in exchange for something of value. Carl provides an introduction to the structure of buzz marketing campaigns and related agency activities, including the ethical concerns about how agents balance their role as buzz agents with their relational role as friends, family members, and co-workers within interactions where issues of trust are critical.

The key findings from the study are that WOM happened most often face-to-face, usually in one of the participants' homes, and was most frequent among friends, demonstrating that relationship type was a factor in interactions. Secondly, WOM was not always positive, which Carl cautions does not necessarily mean that neutral and negative WOM is not effective. Since trust is an important component of an agent's role, honesty may have beneficial implications for the effectiveness of this buzz interaction. The article concludes that WOM is not rooted in traditional, corporate marketing but is, rather, integrally tied to everyday interactions and communication.

Exercise 9.1   Library buzz

How can you put the power of buzz to work in your library?

Additional resources

BzzAgent: *http://www.bzzagent.com* – a word of mouth media network.
Also: 'Anti-buzz agent' posts:

- *http://brandautopsy.typepad.com/brandautopsy/2005/01/ more_bad_bzz_fo.html*
- *http://90days.bzzagent.com/*

Notes

1. Emmanuel Rosen (2000) *The Anatomy of Buzz*. New York: Currency Books, p. 6.
2. Ibid., p. 7.
3. Steve Brooks (2006) 'How to build buzzzzz,' *Restaurant Business*, 105 (11): 30–5.
4. Malcolm Gladwell (2002) *The Tipping Point: How Little Things Can Make a Big Difference*. New York: Little, Brown.
5. Ibid.
6. Seth Godin (2002) *Unleashing the Ideavirus*. New York: Simon & Shuster.
7. Brooks, 'How to build buzzzzz.'
8. Andrew Kaikati and Jack Kaikati (2004) 'Stealth marketing: how to reach customers surreptitiously,' *California Management Review*, 46 (4): 6–22.
9. Ibid.
10. Renée Dye (2000) 'The buzz on buzz,' *Harvard Business Review*, November/December: 145.
11. Ibid., p. 144.

12. Ibid., p. 146.
13. Walter Carl (2006) 'What's all the buzz about? Everyday communication and the relational basis of word-of-mouth and buzz marketing practices,' *Management Communication Quarterly*, 19: 601–34.

Marketing to women

Introduction

Recently in the business press, there has been a discovery that women are, in fact, different from men (!). According to Faith Popcorn, author of the best-selling *The Popcorn Report*, 'women don't buy brands, they join them.' This chapter will explore how this new discovery can increase the effectiveness of your library marketing plan.

Library user statistics

When looking for statistics on female library patrons, I was surprised to find so little information out there. So I enlisted the help of Simmons College's über-librarian Linda Watkins, who was also surprised to find so few statistics on library users. We were able to come up with statistics from a few locales, and there appears to be more tracking (or at least publishing of) library users in countries other than the United States. Most librarians and library directors reported anecdotally that they observed women in their late 20s and 30s, particularly those with children, using their libraries, but not much more was known.

One of the studies that we were able to find, conducted in Pennsylvania, found that the vast majority of library patrons are female (71.5 percent) and homemakers (25.2 percent). Making up the largest age group (25.7 percent) were those between the ages of 35 and 44 while a mere 6.6 percent were between the ages of 18 and 25 (the smallest age group).[1]

In another survey conducted in 44 libraries in the Victoria district of Australia, 68 percent of Library Census respondents were female and 32 percent were male. This compares with 51 percent female and 49 percent male in the Victorian population. Their age categories were a bit different than the Pennsylvania survey, the ages of the lowest patronage being 15–24 years.[2]

Another study, conducted to examine public library use at Loughborough University in the UK, found that 58 percent of library users were female and the smallest age group were people between the ages of 15 and 24 (9 percent).[3]

'So what?' you might be asking. These statistics, and lack thereof, may show that not many libraries are tracking (or sharing) information about their patrons – information that would not only be useful in putting together a marketing plan, but also in determining if the library is meeting its goals and achieving its mission. Also, the statistics seem to indicate that women are more likely to visit the library. It would be interesting to break down the age groups by gender to see if that sheds further light on the male/female breakdown of library users. But since women tend to be in the majority of library users, and this is a marketing book, let's take a look at how men and women differ in their relationships with products and services.

It's a woman's world

In Tom Peter's book *The Circle of Innovation*, he asserts that it's a woman's world. He states: 'It is the R-I-D-I-C-U-L-O-U-S-L-Y rare corporation that takes advantage of the WOMEN'S OPPORTUNITY. What a (COSTLY) mistake.'[4]

Peters cites various surprising statistics to back up his assertions, for example:

- 10.2 million women (20 percent of working wives) make more money than their husbands.

- Women purchase 52 percent ... of tires.

- Women = 43 percent of Americans with assets greater than $500,000.

Peters also declares that American women are, 'in effect, the largest "national" economy on earth ... larger than the entire (!) Japanese economy.'[5]

Peters cites Australian research which discusses the percentage of choices to buy a product that are made or decisively influenced by women:

Home furnishings	94%
Homes	91%
New bank accounts	89%
Medical insurance	88%

One of the issues that Peters presents is that 'Businesses must understand ... first and foremost ... THAT MEN AND WOMEN ARE DIFFERENT.'[6] Not better, not worse, just different. And, as will be discussed later in this chapter, women buy for different reasons and respond differently to marketing messages.

Peters asserts that Sears finally got the message. He

quotes Arthur Martinez, the chair and CEO of Sears, Roebuck & Co.:

> We had a company run by guys who thought they were in the 'dirty fingernails' business with autos and hardware. Unless we made the store and merchandise attractive to women, we weren't going to break out of the box we were in. It was a very big 'ah-ha' discovery.[7]

Peters credits Sears' turnaround to reinventing the store and catering to women.

Recently, American Airlines has tried to capture the women's market. On their website, the company has placed special links to cater to women travelers. From the website:

> We've listened to women and recognized the need to provide additional information tailored to your business and pleasure travel needs and lifestyle. We also invite you to share insights, travel tips and stories by submitting them to us.

The links for women include 'women connected through business,' 'women connected through lifestyle,' and 'women connected through each other.' There are additional links including 'girlfriend getaways' and 'family fun.'[8]

American Airlines went so far as to create a special women's search box (for searching for flights). The box was originally pink and had several options for customizing flights. American quickly revised this search box, presumably from negative feedback.[9]

In order to capitalize on marketing to women, Peters suggests starting by asking six questions:

1. What share of your sales is attributable to women?

2. How ... specifically ... do women's tastes influence your product development, sales, marketing, logistics, and service in your company?

3. What percentage of senior people ... are women?

4. Is anyone ... doing a fabulous job (à la Sears) catering to women?

5 How big is the 'women's opportunity' in your segments?

6. Do you have an explicit women's strategy that involves the marketing and the organizational capability associated with serving it imaginatively?

Peters cautions 'DO NOT ACCEPT SUPERFICIAL ANSWERS TO ANY OF THESE QUESTIONS!'[10]

Exercise 10.1   The 'woman's thing' @ your library

Relate Peters' questions above to your library – do you know any of the answers? If not, how can you collect this information?

Has your library EVE-olved?

In her book *EVEolution,* Faith Popcorn puts forth eight 'truths' for marketing to women:

1. Connecting your female customers to each other connects them to your brand.

2. If you're marketing to one of her lives, you're missing all the others.

3. If she has to ask, it's too late.

4. Market to her peripheral vision and she will see you in a whole new light.

5. Walk, run, go to her, secure her loyalty forever.

6. This generation of women customers will lead you to the next.

7. Co-parenting is the best way to raise a brand.

8. Everything matters – you can't hide behind your logo.[11]

Six of the truths are described as follows.

Connect

Popcorn asserts that women are great connectors – she gives the example: 'A woman sits down to dinner at a restaurant and by the time the glass of wine arrives, she knows the name of the waiter's acting coach and the next play he has a part in.'[12] She argues that this is not gossip, but the fundamental way women think and behave – that we need to link with one another and 'cross-pollinate.' So what does this mean for marketing? Popcorn cites Lori Moskowitz, founder of the Intuition Group, which discovered that women are three times as likely to recommend products that they know their friends are looking for. Additionally, Popcorn cites another market research group that did a survey showing 70 percent of women believe that they learn the most about a product from someone who already owns it. Popcorn provides additional ammunition by referring to connections made by Oprah, Weight Watchers, iVillage, Oxygen, and many others. She concludes by stating: 'Women don't buy brands, they join them.'[13]

Market to multiple lives

The second 'truth,' according to Popcorn, revolves around the research that Helen Fisher, author of *The First Sex*, found: 'Men do one thing at a time, while women do many things at the same time.'[14] Popcorn suggests that women are born multitaskers, even going so far as to suggest that women have a variation of Attention Deficit Disorder – that we cannot filter out distractions. Fisher states that if a man is watching TV with the radio on reading a newspaper, he is actually compartmentalizing each activity and switching from one to another in his brain. Women cannot ignore two of the three and end up with sensory overload. Popcorn believes that women are able to do several things at one time – and do them well. The multiple roles women assume is of particular value to marketers. Women look for products and services that allow them to do several tasks at once and juggle their many different roles. The trick here, according to Popcorn, is to appeal to the many different roles women assume rather then focusing on just one (for example mother, wife, educator, etc.).[15]

Asking too late

Popcorn asserts women never actually ask for what they want, so marketers have to anticipate the needs of women. This sounds a bit of a Catch-22; however, Popcorn states that marketers can avoid problems if they include women in the planning process.[16]

Catch her peripheral vision

According to Popcorn, women don't respond to 'in your face' advertising. She attributes this to, as in the second truth, the fact that women respond to information differently than men. 'Women don't just look at the center ring of the bull's eye – we look around it, walk around it, circle around it.' For example, women are far more likely to seek out a Talbots suit that Katie Couric wore on the evening news than if that same suit is advertised by Talbots in a television commercial on the same station.

Popcorn also uses the example of Starbucks as a brand that successfully markets to the peripheral vision of women. Due in part to the lack of funding for advertising, Starbucks instead focused on creating value and good customer service, which caught the attention of women (60 percent of Starbuck's customers are female). Popcorn asserts that Starbucks' biggest triumphs in peripheral marketing were its alliance with Barnes & Noble bookstores and Oprah's Book Club to sell her selections in their cafés. 'By appealing to the female customer in an entirely different and extremely attractive context – stress-free, with books to browse through – Starbucks has extended its reach beyond the storefront café.' Marketing to the peripheral vision takes time and needs to be well thought out, according to Popcorn. She says: 'Be subtle, be clever, be consistent.'[17]

Secure her loyalty

This truth revolves around the busy pace most women live their lives at. By going to her, rather than her having to go to you, Popcorn states, you will win her loyalty. Not only does this truth involve home delivery, but also making it easy for her to find you (not only your physical location, but also making your website easy to navigate). Popcorn includes ideas for small tanker trucks to pull up to your house to fill up your car rather than you having to drive to the gas station, a BabyGap van that pulls up to the pediatrician's office … the opportunities are almost endless.[18]

Generational marketing

Popcorn asserts that mothers are the primary filter of all things in life so 'it seems obvious that a woman's buying habits would be greatly influenced by what her mother bought.'[19] And while there is no guarantee that daughters will always choose products that their mother bought, it is much easier for marketers to get though the clutter of other brands. Popcorn terms this tendency as 'Brand-Me-Down.' Popcorn gives the following advice for this truth to marketers:

> You need to see where all your intergenerational strengths and weaknesses are. You can then develop a strategy that focuses on the bonds that exist through all stages of life. Childhood, college, first apartment, career, early years of marriage, parenthood, second career, retirement. The key is to look along the branches of a woman's family tree for marketing opportunities.[20]

In 2003, Marti Barletta wrote in her book *Marketing to Women: How to Understand, Reach, and Increase Your Share of the World's Largest Market Segment*:

> Women are the world's most powerful consumers. They are the big spenders, whether you're talking about households, corporate purchasing, or small businesses. Would you believe that there is *not a single book* that addresses the nuts-and-bolts specifics of how to market to persons of the female persuasion? Sure ... there are plenty of books that focus on much smaller markets with a lot less money – kids' marketing, Gen X marketing ... And yet, until now there has been not one book that ... details specific marketing tactics for the consumer group that

marketers need most: women. What's the first rule of marketing? Understand your market. The second rule? Understand your customer.[21]

Barletta continues by stating:

> Up until now, we assumed that men and women operated pretty much the same way when it comes to buying decisions. We thought the marketing maxims ... were 'normal' for all adults. Upon closer examination, it's turning out that they're normal for *men*. Women have a pretty different set of priorities, preferences, and attitudes. Their purchase-decision process is radically different. And they respond differently to marketing media and messages, language and visuals.[22]

As far as marketing messages are concerned, Barletta argues that men tend to reduce marketing messages to the bare details when women need more detail. She states:

> In their view, details not only add to richness and depth but are necessary to an understanding of the situation. How can you possibly grasp the big picture without a detailed knowledge of the specifics? How can you appreciate the real issues without a thorough familiarity with the context? Women look to add information, not cut it away.[23]

Exercise 10.2   Sending marketing messages

How can you apply Barletta's ideas to your library's marketing program?

Notes

1. Charles McClure and John Carlo Bertot (1998) 'Public library use in Pennsylvania: identifying uses, benefits, and impacts,' Pennsylvania Department of Education, Office of Commonwealth Libraries, and the Bureau of Library Development, available at: *http://www.ii.fsu.edu/~cmcclure/padeptedumerge.pdf* (accessed 29 July 2007).
2. See: *http://www.slv.vic.gov.au/pdfs/aboutus/publications/lbcreport1_2006.pdf* (accessed 17 July 2007).
3. See: *http://www.lboro.ac.uk/departments/dis/lisu/lampost06/users06.html#plugengr* (accessed 17 July 2007).
4. Tom Peters (1999) *Circle of Innovation: You Can't Shrink Your Way to Greatness.* New York: Vintage Books, p. 395.
5. Ibid., p. 400.
6. Ibid.
7. Ibid., p. 414.
8. See: *http://www.aa.com/women* (accessed 17 July 2007).
9. *http://www.consumerist.com/consumer/american-airlines/american-airlines-alters-adorable-pink-womens-search-box-251880.php*
10. Peters, *Circle of Innovation*, p. 422.
11. Faith Popcorn (2000) *EVEolution: The Eight Truths of Marketing to Women.* New York: Hyperion.
12. Ibid., p. 18.
13. Ibid., p. 39.
14. Helen Fisher (1999) *The First Sex: The Natural Talents of Women and How They Are Changing the World.* New York: Ballantine.
15. Popcorn, *EVEolution*, p. 42.
16. Ibid., p. 80.
17. Ibid., p. 125.
18. Ibid., p. 140.
19. Ibid., p. 154.
20. Ibid., p. 174.
21. Marti Barletta (2003) *Marketing to Women: How to Understand, Reach, and Increase Your Share of the World's Largest Market Segment.* New York: Dearborn Trade Publishing, p. xix.

22. Ibid., p. xxi.
23. Ibid., p. 67.

11

Marketing to Millennials

Introduction

In order to effectively market a service, product, or company, it is critical to consider the facets of consumers to whom you intend to target the marketing. Target marketing is the practice of identifying a primary audience for a product based on one or more characteristics which they have in common. This chapter will discuss a common problem for many libraries – attracting Millennials to the library.

Background

The emergence of modern target marketing can be traced to a 1964 article by Dik Warren Twedt titled 'How important to marketing strategy is the "heavy user"?'[1] This article was an early look at how different segments of a population have different purchasing and product use trends. This marked a shift from traditional mass marketing strategies in place before this time. In 1984, researchers Cook and Mindak tested to see if Twedt's findings held true twenty years later, and they found they did. Over forty years after

Twedt's research was published, the marketing industry is heavily committed to the principles and practice of target marketing.[2]

When Twedt wrote his article in the 1960s, marketing to young children and teenagers was not commonplace. Products intended for this group were typically targeted at mothers who made the majority of purchasing decisions for their family. However, over the subsequent four decades, marketers have increasingly had opportunities to interact with children without parental mediation, such as unsupervised television viewing and Internet use. This has resulted in a dramatic increase in the amount and sophistication of marketing to this target audience. The reciprocal effect of the spending influence and power of this target market has also emerged.

Millennials are generally defined as those born between 1982 and 2002. Also referred to as the Net Generation, Echo Boomers, Generation Y, and Generation Why, the Millennial label refers to the year when the first wave of people in this generation graduated from high school. They can generally be described as being tech savvy and team orientated, and having high levels of achievement and idealism, high expectations for fame and fortune, and connectedness to peers through technology anytime and anywhere. This group has unprecedented levels of attention from marketers, especially as they continue to mature, increase their income and make larger and different purchasing decisions.

Issues and concerns

Kotler cautions that marketers should be careful to define the target market carefully and to distinguish between different audiences when developing marketing materials.[3] While a product might appeal to a broad audience, for marketing purposes it is important to identify market segments to target your marketing to and to understand who your target is, such as where they live, what they buy, when they buy, where they spend time, etc. It is important to understand what interests and motivates this group, whose concerns are influenced heavily by social and technological change, so marketers can anticipate (and steer) shifts in the target. Successfully communicating the benefits of your product to the primary audience for your product increases the chances the product will be successful. It is also advantageous from an economic standpoint to increase the potential for a higher return on investment for marketing and advertising dollars spent.

Technology and analytics allow marketers to gain insights into customer behaviors in online interactions, a practice called *behavioral targeting*. According to eMarketer, behavioral targeting in online advertising will be a $1.5 billion segment of the marketing industry in 2007. Behavioral targeting has emerged as a powerful and highly effective segmentation strategy. It is based on the psychographic factors of how, when, and under what circumstances a customer uses the product, but also takes that information and deduces the likes and dislikes of the audience based on their behaviors.

Resource Interactive, an interactive agency based in Columbus, Ohio, has conducted qualitative and quantitative research on what they call 'Digital Millennials.' In their November 2006 newsletter *Litmus*, Resource Interactive defines Millennials based on their connectedness to each other through and in virtual worlds, their ability to multitask and simultaneously filter out irrelevant messages, and the observation that they are more trusting of peers than authority figures and are self-expressive and optimistic.[4]

The resulting analysis conducted by Resource Interactive and JupiterResearch provides guideposts to understanding the motivations behind the actions and lifestyle of this target market. The critical traits the Millennial market seeks in a brand are: authenticity and freshness; companies that listen to customers; creative and limited-duration incentives; personalization and control; and entertainment, news, and stories.

Resource Interactive continues by defining how to market to this target market: (1) stimulate; (2) engage; (3) purchase; and (4) empower and re-engage. Marketers who embrace this modern purchasing model will reap the rewards, they suggest. 'Tech savvy, multitasking and optimistic, they are ready to delivery economic opportunity to brands that make the effort to engage them – and their social networks – as equals in the brand experience.'[5]

Alex Spunt of *Adweek* defines Millennials as an evolving group that is increasingly DIY (do-it-yourself) with unlimited access to information. They are hard to impress – preferring to learn from their peers than from authority figures. Her position is that buzz marketing will be the most effective marketing strategy to apply to this target market. She explains that 'any brand actively targeting a youth market is probably making a mistake because for them a strong product may be better off with little to no marketing.' The issue of DIY brands such as MySpace, YouTube, and Flickr illustrate the success of directly involving the audience in the content and community, noting that voyeurism adds to authenticity. Another example Spunt provides is that of J Brand jeans, which found success with the launch its line of high-end jeans ($150–$225 a pair) by benefiting from the buzz generated as a result of celebrities wearing the product. The brand did very little initial advertising, but has been highly successful, selling in upscale bricks and mortar boutiques and through numerous online retailers.[6]

Niche marketing is a strategy that a marketer may use to further narrow their market. Niches break down the primary market segments into even more narrowly defined groups based on specific needs. Niche marketing allows the marketer, and thereby the company, to have a closer relationship with the niche audience, and can demonstrate a company's dedication to the particular target market. Applying the strategy of niche marketing can be highly successful, but it has its risks. If your niche market weakens, your marketing effort does too. In order to reduce the risks associated with niches, marketers often employ multiniches which group two or more niches together. If one niche softens, the overall impact to the campaign is not as severe as if there had been only one niche.[7]

While niches may not be an advantageous strategy to use with the relatively unstable and emerging Millennial demographic, it should be noted that there are many individual niche identities within this generational label. *Brand Strategy* magazine conducted qualitative research to identify nine 'tribes' of the Millennial demographic, each representing between 6 and 18 percent of the whole. The largest group, Moshers (18 percent of the target audience), are highly independent, question authority, are not label conscious, have strong values, and place high importance on authenticity. Other tribes are Socialites (11 percent) who are ostentatiously materialistic, Cool Geeks (17 percent) who are aspirational, Sporties (10 percent) who are energetic, competitive, and influenced by sports, and Chavs (9 percent) who are materialistic but prefer not to stand out.[8]

Features

Millennials are more digitally native than any group before them. All Millennials (by date of birth demographics) were born after the first personal computers became available. They are online more often than not, and have multiple devices and preferences for communicating with peers and finding information. The independence that has emerged from the virtually unfettered access to information and each other poses an interesting challenge to marketers. What are the best ways to enter their circle? What tools are the best to use when communicating with Millennials?

Trend School is the monthly one-day forum organized by Creative Artists Association. It provides marketers with a chance to become immersed in the Millennial mindset by interacting with a panel of 16–25 year olds. The general messages are not surprising – 'cool in context' and 'what's in it for me?' – but what is interesting are the insights into the Millennial world. The Trend School panelists have offered suggestions ranging from companies offering widgets that use RSS to deliver information to DIY mashups (the practice of taking existing materials or data and creating a new use for it) such as Ikeahacker.blogspot.com where users share creative repurposing of Ikea products.[9]

Noting the challenges raised by this target market, marketers are selecting promotional tie-ins that carefully entice (and not repel) the target. One example of this is Subway's 2006 summer tie-in with Vans. Subway wanted to increase its appeal to tweens (8–12 year olds) and teens (13–17 year olds), capitalizing on messages teens hear about healthy eating in schools. While acknowledging that teens are not motivated to make healthy eating choices on their own, Subway wanted to position itself as an easy way for them to eat healthily. They know that many teens come to

Subway without being targeted. Teens (in focus groups) said they trust the Subway brand, 'because sandwiches are made in front of customers' and 'they don't care if you are a picky eater.' Their research into the demographic told them that Vans was seen as an authentic brand. Mirroring the sensibilities of the demographic, Michelle Cordial, marketing director for the Subway brand, said: 'We were looking for a lifestyle brand, not necessarily sports properties.' Vans was the brand that matched their goals.[10]

Traditional marketing doesn't work with this target market as reliably as it has for other groups. They are hard to reach both because of their sense of individuality and their generally non-mainstream focus. They are conditioned to be constantly connected and adaptable. On the one hand it is helpful to know they are always online, but on the other their uses of technology are not consistent. Their sense of trust and peer influence has led to the practice of formalized 'buzz' marketing (see Chapter 9 for more on buzz). Buzz agencies now train and compensate buzz agents to spread buzz about a product or service in their everyday interactions with their peer group. Knowing the influence of word-of-mouth on product use and purchases, the marketing industry has created the process and framework to disseminate messages peer to peer.[11]

Related issues

There are three significant areas of tangential interest and impact related to marketing to the Millennial generation. The first is that the buying and spending influence of this generation is substantial. Second, is the practice of and identity relating to mashups – the practice of taking assets intended for one use and reusing them for another purpose.

And finally there is the tangential health and safety issue of obesity, how it impacts this generation and will have delayed but serious impact on the prosperity, needs, and concerns of this target market.

The Millennial generation holds significant sway in the purchasing and spending habits of their families. At nearly 100 million strong, this generation is larger than the Baby Boomers, the sweethearts of marketers until recently. Kelly Mooney, an online marketing expert, reports that this group is 'involved in 81% of apparel selection and 52% of car choices.' Their preferences for individuality and need for immediacy will drive the wholesale reworking of websites and the introduction of new services. Their collective spending potential is enormous. Marketers will continue to focus on this market as they establish careers and make larger spending choices for themselves.[12]

Not only do Millennial consumers want to personalize their buying experience and purchases, but they also want to create an individual identity with a brand. Marketers should continue to provide opportunities for customers (in this case mostly Millennials) to do just that. Encouraging users to repurpose branded media and distribute it will provide viral, peer-influenced marketing. In a shift from traditional brand ownership, marketers should embrace the creativity and ingenuity of this target audience.

According to a survey on childhood obesity by the Mercury News/Kaiser Family Foundation (14 March 2004):

> 15 percent of children and teens aged 6–19 are overweight and another 15% are at risk of becoming overweight. An estimated 80% of overweight adolescents continue to be obese into adulthood. Obesity in the United States has been labeled an epidemic by the Centers for Disease Control and Prevention.

The impact on the nation's health care and on the overall health of the Millennial generation is significant.[13]

A separate report from Kaiser on the role of the media in childhood obesity reviews over 40 studies on the topic to identify what researchers know and do not know about their relationship. Children spend an average of five-and-a-half hours a day in front of screen media, much of it targeted marketing for unhealthy foods (fast food, soda, and snacks). Whatever the correlation between media habits and obesity (much more remains to be researched and written on the topic), it is generally agreed that issues of physical activity displaced by media use, snacking while watching, body image depictions, and cross-promotions of food products and media personalities can contribute to childhood obesity.[14]

Alternatives

Millennials are a hard to reach target, but not because they are a particularly difficult group of people. The challenge in reaching them is that their lifestyles are in sync with the changing technology they use and help define. The target is independent, connected, busy, and puts more value into individualized, low-to-no promotion efforts than they do to hard-sell, mainstream messages. While they may seem elusive, Millennials are accessible, if you go to them.

Reaching Millennials requires a complete reworking of marketing strategy. They have the technology skills and savvy to embrace or reject online marketing efforts, and the value placed on peer recommendations makes a mention in an influential blog a victory for a marketer. While it seems a somewhat haphazard hope that word-of-mouth marketing works for the target, marketers are leaving little to chance but engaging 'buzz' marketing agencies which apply appropriate methods and processes to building and spreading product buzz. It is important to consider that Millennials are generally drawn to fun, interactive opportunities, and that they look to influential peers for direction instead of authority figures.

While some marketers have had success targeting the Millennial generation, most are catching up. Marketers must think creatively, anticipate technology and communication trends, and listen to Millennial consumers, and thus should be able to bridge this awkward period of struggling to reach the target market.

Relevance

Millennials are an enormous population that libraries service today, and as they age, they will become the graduate students and faculty of the academic community and the parents and patrons of the public library system. Libraries are also not traditionally early adopters or quick adapters to new thinking and strategies, although libraries are typically technologically up to date. For example, the Millennial target market is developing and using widgets that use RSS to deliver information, such as putting a Library Thing (*http://www.librarything.com*) widget in their MySpace profile.[15]

There are many target market drivers for libraries to consider in addressing the Millennial generation's need for physical spaces, online offerings, finding aids, program offerings and customer service. Based on a three-year study by Net Day on student and teacher views of technology and education, among other factors, Millennials want support for learning technical skills, such as software, and they have a preference for self-service web access and learning.[16] The ECAR *Study of Undergraduate Students and Information Technology 2006*[17] validates this latter finding, noting that undergraduate students have high expectations for mobility and access to IT. Additionally, as the concerns of a 'digital divide' in the United States make way for the challenge of the 'participation gap,' patrons will look to the library as the source only after they cannot find it freely online. Pew Internet and American Life Project's *Internet Penetration and Impact Memo*[18] speaks to this, noting that it is increasingly common for patrons to use publicly available search engines as the first step in researching a topic before going to a library resource.

The impact on the relevance of the library to this community makes understanding the wants and needs of this target market tantamount to the success of libraries, both academic and public. As we look forward, the Millennial target is expected to have continued high expectations for self-service access to information and learning; flexibility in the library as a place (group study places, comfortable places to work individually and as an individual with friends); enforced policies for cell phones and noise; flexibility in access to information, service, and support on demand; and transparent technical infrastructure both in the library and through remote access, including wireless support, loaner laptops, and ease of printing.

Conclusions

The Millennial target market is large and will have a significant impact on dominant spending and buying trends and the overall United States economy as it ages. The spending power of teens is impressive. According to 360 Youth Marketing (now alloy media + marketing), 'One in three high school seniors carry a credit card and as a group they earn 63% of their income independently from parents and spend it on brands they know and trust.'[19] Their marketing and advertising savvy, plus their adaptability to new products and innovation, have made them an unfamiliar market for marketers. Marketers have responded with new analytics from web and user testing and formalized 'buzz' marketing strategies. While their age demographic has been a key identifier of the target, the core traits are hard to pin down, but can be grouped by niche. On the niche level, marketers will find more success delivering an intended message to the audience. Marketers recognize the level of transparency Millennials expect, and have tapped into that target desire by making companies appear more accessible.

The future – the impact of change and what lies ahead

Looking forward at anticipated trends in marketing to the Millennial target market, there will likely be an emphasis on niche marketing and a new economic model for customers to purchase and use the product.

With regard to niche marketing, the industry should anticipate more multicultural marketing of teenagers by ethnic background. Marketers will have to address who the spokespeople are for brands and ensure that they reflect the targeted niche. One likely avenue for this is through carefully selected 'buzz' marketing agents to influence customers. Just as Millennials are a large and attractive target market, so are the multicultural markets, such as the rapidly growing Hispanic market (44.7 million people).

However, it is possible that as 'buzz' marketing becomes more sophisticated and widespread, it could have an unintended backlash. The perceived abuse of trusted relationships raises ethical questions from a marketing standpoint, but will likely have a negative impact on marketing once consumers recognize the practice exists.[20]

New business models lie ahead as well. Piczo, a service similar to Flickr, is looking towards a move from a 100 percent advertising revenue model to e-tail (electronic retail). Customers are now able to add small amounts of money to a card to make purchases, such as popular store cards and the widely used PayPal accounts. The use of these tools will likely result in an easing of criticism of the credit and security issues related to young people and spending money online, and likely drive younger consumers to make more purchases for and by themselves. In a development that suggests what lies ahead for the changing business landscape, Newscorp (which owns MySpace, among a plethora of newspaper and broadcast entities) bought Jamster (e-tailer of cell phone ring tones and wallpaper) in Fall 2006. It seems obvious that connecting MySpace users with a preferred cell accessory partner is a good business match-up. The forecast of a decade ago that micro-payments would drive web purchasing activity may be coming to fruition. The Millennial target market has already adopted this practice with $2.99 ring tones and $0.99 songs on iTunes.[21]

There will be more common use of behavioral targeting as technology allows marketers to personalize messages to customers, for example the highly rich and targeted advertisements such as the Mini Cooper personalized billboards based on signals sent by a customer's key fob. Another example is how Snapple found consumers for a new green tea product. Originally targeted to people with health and fitness lifestyles, when tested the target was identified as 'those interested in arts and literature' and 'people who traveled internationally.' The process of researching consumer behavior can hold surprises, especially because sometimes a marketer or company doesn't know what questions to ask.

Briefly, there are three other areas where marketers will likely focus their attentions. First is the possible placement of marketing in areas where Millennials spend time, such as Second Life and other virtual worlds. Second will be the investment in digital video distributed online. And finally, there will be a shift in the focus of how marketers approach the relationship with their customers – providing more direct communication with consumers in order to hear what they have to say and also to give the customer a voice.

Exercise 11.1   **Marketing to Millennials**

How can you use the information from this chapter to better market your library to Millennials? What additional ideas can you come up with? Compare your thoughts with the following list.

Millennial marketing ideas

- Digital message board in elementary school cafeteria
- Miniature golf course on library grounds
- Networking with elementary school teachers and administrators to get program flyers in mailboxes
- Technology – using podcasts, IM, e-mail, library website to reach them

Notes

1. Dik Warren Twedt (1964) 'How important to marketing strategy is the "heavy user"?' *Journal of Marketing*, 28(1): 71–2.

2. Victor Cook Jr and William Mindak (1984) 'A search for constants: the "heavy use"' revisited!,' *Journal of Consumer Marketing*, 4: 79–81.

3. Philip Kotler (1999) *Kotler on Marketing: How to Create, Win, and Dominate Markets*. New York: Free Press, p. 173.

4. Resource Interactive (2006) 'Decoding the digital Millennials: large in number, huge in influence,' *Litmus*, November.

5. Ibid., p. 10.

6. Alex Spunt (2006) 'Take a cue from teens,' *Adweek*, 47: 15.

7. Kotler, *Kotler on Marketing*, p. 27.

8. Michael Watt and John Cliff, 'Teen spirit: research teenage tribes,' *Brand Strategy*, March: 44–5.

9. Beth Bulik (2007) 'Want to build a hipper brand? Take a trip to trend school,' *Advertising Age*, 78: 3–64.

10. Betsy Spethmann (2006) 'Subway freshens kids marketing: Vans tie-in drives summer action for kids, tweens,' *Promo*, July.

11. Walter Carl (2006) 'What's all the buzz about? Everyday communication and the relational basis of word-of-mouth and buzz marketing practices,' *Management Communication Quarterly*, 19: 601–34.

12. Abbey Klaassen (2007) 'Behavioral targeting: the new killer app for research,' *Advertising Age*, 78: 17.

13. San Jose Mercury News/Kaiser Family Foundation (2004) *Survey on Childhood Obesity: Summary Document and Chartpack*, available at: *http://www.kff.org/kaiserpolls/upload/Survey-on-Childhood-Obesity-Summary-and-Chartpack.pdf* (accessed 31 July 2007).

14. Kaiser Family Foundation (2004) *The Role of Media in Childhood Obesity*. Available at: *http://www.kff.org/entmedia/7030.cfm* (accessed 27 January 2008).

15. Cathy De Rosa, Joanne Cantrell, Diane Cellentani, Janet Hawk, Lillie Jenkins, and Alane Wilson (2005) *Perceptions of Libraries and Information Resources: A Report to the OCLC Membership*. Dublin, OH: OCLC.

16. Available at: *http://www.tomorrow.org/speakup/pdf/ speakupreport_05.pdf* (accessed 28 January 2008).

17. Gail Salaway, Richard Katz, Judith Caruso, Robert Kvavik, and Mark Nelson (2006) *The ECAR Study of Undergraduate Students and Information Technology 2006*, Vol. 7. Boulder, CO: ECAR.

18. Mary Madden (2006) *Internet Penetration and Impact.* Pew Internet & American Life Project, available at: *http:// pewinternet.org/pdfs/PIP_Internet-Impact.pdf*

19. *360 Youth Marketing* (2007), available at: *http://www .alloymarketing.com/media/teens/index.html* (accessed 28 January 2008).

20. Doug Wintz (2007) *The Ethics of Behavioral Targeting*, available at: *http://www.imediaconnection.com/content/ 13902.asp* (accessed 31 July 2007).

21. Andrew McCormick (2006) 'Piczo to sell to teenage users in move away from ad-only model,' *New Media Age*, 28 September.

12

Marketing yourself

Introduction

The final chapter of this book focuses on you and your career. In the book *Now Discover Your Strengths*, Marcus Buckingham and Donald Clifton based their research on a Gallup poll of 198,000 employees. They asked the question: 'At work, do you have the opportunity to do what you do best every day?' The people who agreed worked in organizations with low turnover, high productivity, and high customer satisfaction scores.[1] Unfortunately, as you might have guessed, the number that responded positively that their strengths were truly in play every day was a mere 20 percent. If you are in the other 80 percent, this chapter is for you.

Are you remarkable?

In Seth Godin's *Purple Cow*, he describes the typical job search strategy – sending out résumés and/or posting them online, and the like – as 'nothing but advertising.' And as he discusses in the book, advertising by itself is not very effective. The other way to get a job is to be remarkable.

'Remarkable people with remarkable careers seem to switch jobs with far less effort. Remarkable people often do not even have a résumé … remarkable people are often recruited from jobs they love to jobs they love even more.'[2] He continues: 'If you're thinking about being a Purple Cow, the time to do it is when you're not looking for a job. In your career, even more than for a brand, being safe is risky. The path to lifetime job security is to be remarkable.'[3]

In *Free Prize Inside*, Godin states: 'Being engaged at work is seductive. It means you're spending a big chunk of every day doing something you love, something that makes a difference. You get to motivate other people and create things that last. Unfortunately, this sort of opportunity is scarce, and (apparently) getting even more scarce.' He further explains: 'Since your boss hired you to make something happen, you now have permission to build a free prize. You have the opportunity (on your bosses nickel) to build a project that will energize you and your co-workers.'[4] He also states that while creating 'free prize' projects in your organization isn't hard, it is difficult to be a champion and get them accepted. He further argues: 'Difficult work is easy to avoid. Difficult work is exactly what will get you promoted.'[5] He brings up some very good points.

In *Fish!*, Stephen Lundin, Harry Paul, and John Christensen identify the elements for improving morale and results in organizations which were gleaned from the Pike Place Fish Market in Seattle Washington. These include: 'Choose Your Attitude,' 'Play,' 'Make Their Day,' and 'Be Present.'[6]

The authors state that one of the things we have the most control over each day is that attitude we take to our jobs. We may not have control over what else we do, but we can choose our attitude. They point out: 'When you are you doing what you are doing, who are you being? Are you being impatient and bored or are you being world famous? You are going to act differently when you are being world famous.'[7] The idea of being world famous is also echoed in Tom Peters' *Circle of Innovation*, where he argues that we are all 'Michelangelos.' He writes: '"Can you imagine," a hotel manager once asked me, "Michelangelos of housekeeping?" Then he added "If you can't, you ought to get the hell out of the hospitality business."' Peters continues: 'MICHELANGELOS OF HOUSEKEEPING. YES I L-O-V-E THAT! What about Michelangelos of parking ... Michelangelos of accounts receivable? Michelangelos of plumbing ... Michelangelos of hairstyling? Michelangelos of —? (You fill in the blanks.)'[8] OK then, what about Michelangelos of reference? Tech services? Circulation? Choose to come to work with your Michelangelo attitude.

The second component of the *Fish!* philosophy is Fun: Fun is energizing – how can you have more of it at work? The third component is Making Their Day: the Pike Place workers engage their customers and include them in their good time. How can you make your patrons' day? The last component is Being Present – the Pike Place guys constantly scan the crowd and interact with their customers. They are not talking on cell phones or daydreaming.[9]

Exercise 12.1   Go fishin'

How can you put the Fish! *philosophy to work at your library?*

147

Component	How you can put it to work
Choose Your Attitude	
Play	
Make Their Day	
Be Present	

Find your inner hedgehog

In Jim Collins' best-selling book *Good to Great*, he describes what he terms 'the hedgehog concept.' The idea gets its name from the Greek parable, 'The fox knows many things, but the hedgehog knows one big thing.'[10] The fox knows many different ways to try to eat the hedgehog, but when the hedgehog rolls up into a ball each time the fox attacks, the hedgehog wins. According to Collins, 'To be clear, hedgehogs are not stupid. Quite the contrary. They understand the essence of profound insight is simplicity … Hedgehogs see what is essential and ignore the rest.'[11] Collins believes it is essential for us to understand our own hedgehog concept – which he believes to be at the intersection of three concepts he visualizes as three intersecting circles. The first circle represents 'what you can be the best in the world at (and equally important, what you cannot be the best in the world at).' The second circle is what drives your economic engine, and the third what you are passionate about. Collins states:

Suppose you were able to construct a work life that meets the following three tests. First, you are doing work for which you have a genetic or God-given talent, and perhaps you could become the best in the world in applying the talent. ('I feel that I was just born to be doing this.') Second, you are well paid for what you do. ('I get paid to do this? Am I dreaming?') Third, you are doing work you are passionate about and absolutely love to do, enjoying the actual process for its own sake. ('I look forward to getting up and throwing myself into my daily work, and I really believe in what I'm doing.') If you could drive toward the intersection of the three circles and translate that intersection into a simple, crystalline concept guided by your life choices, then you'd have a hedgehog concept for yourself.[12]

Clearly, knowing your hedgehog concept is a key step in marketing yourself to the right organization for the right position.

Exercise 12.2   **Where is your hedgehog?**

Draw three circles on a piece of paper, and label them with each of the hedgehog components. What is your hedgehog concept? Does it match your job? How could it? What do you need to do?

Be a Fred

In Mark Sanborn's book *The Fred Factor*, he recounts the story of his mailman Fred as the inspiration for the text. He describes Fred as the type of person that always goes the extra mile. Some examples: Fred personally took an interest in Sanborn's extensive travel schedule to ensure that mail did not build up in his mailbox while he was away since it might attract burglars; Fred hid a package that came while Sanborn was traveling under the doormat and pushed it to a corner of the porch; Fred picked up a package sent to Sanborn by UPS that was delivered to a neighbor's address and redelivered it to Sanborn; and the list goes on. Of course, Sanborn is not the only person on Fred's delivery route – he treats all the people with the same exceptional customer service. Fred even drives around the neighborhood when he is off duty to chat with the people on his route – taking a personal interest in all of his 'clients.'[13]

Sanborn distills the essence of Fred into 'The Fred Principles': Everyone Makes a Difference; Success is Built on Relationships; You Must Continually Create Value for Others, and It Doesn't Have to Cost a Penny; and You Can Reinvent Yourself Regularly.

Everyone Makes a Difference

Sanborn states that it doesn't matter how big or efficient the organization is, the individual can make a difference. Ultimately, Sanborn states, 'only the employee can choose to do his or her job in an extraordinary way, regardless of the circumstances … Nobody can prevent you from choosing to be exceptional.'[14]

Success Is Built on Relationships

Sanborn explains that the service was superior from Fred because of his relationship with him. 'Indifferent people deliver impersonal service. Service becomes personalized when a relationship exists between the provider and the customer.'[15] Are you developing relationships with your patrons? Many libraries are now instituting employee recommendations for books in an effort to encourage these relationships. Sanborn further generalizes this concept:

- Leaders succeed when they realize their employees are human.

- Technology succeeds when it recognizes that its users are human.

- Employees like Fred the Postman succeed when they recognize their work involves interacting with human beings.[16]

You Must Continually Create Value for Others, and It Doesn't Have to Cost a Penny

This idea is illustrated by Sanborn though the myth of lack of resources. He states that many of us believe that we can't be exceptional because we lack the resources to do so. He debunks this myth through the use of Fred, who did not have any resource at all – except his imagination. Sanborn further explains: 'The faster you try to solve a problem with money, the less likely it will be the best solution. With enough money, anyone can buy his or her way out of a problem. The challenge is to outthink rather than outspend the competition.'[17] So if you think you (or your library) just doesn't have the money to market itself, think (literally) again!

You Can Reinvent Yourself Regularly

Sanborn states that if someone like Fred can put so much creativity and inspiration into putting mail into a box, why can't we reinvent the way we do our jobs? Thinking about the real-life Freds can inspire us to be innovative about doing our jobs. Sanborn gives various examples throughout the text of other 'Freds' in different organizations to illustrate his concepts.

Exercise 12.3   How can you be a Fred?

Think about ways you can use the Fred factor by filling in the chart below:

Everyone Makes a Difference	
Success Is Built on Relationships	
You Must Continually Create Value for Others, and It Doesn't Have to Cost a Penny	
You Can Reinvent Yourself Regularly	

Brand yourself

Oprah. Madonna. Martha. MJ. Are they people or brands? Tom Peters states:

> I am as good as my next gig. (Period.) (Just as a housepainter is. And Harrison Ford.) I grow ... or

perish. (Professionally). And I like that. And I think it is quintessentially American ... Dilbert may label me Goody Two Shoes or Mr. Rose Colored Glasses. But Ben Franklin – our first 'self-help guru' – would get it.[18]

Additionally, Peters believes we should all think and act like independent contractors, even if we plan to stay on the organization's payroll. 'An Independent Contractor is self-reliant. Dependent on her-his skills ... and the constant upgrading thereof. An Independent Contractor has ... in the end ... "only" her-his Track Record.'[19] He calls this Independent Contractor 'Brand You ... A brand is shorthand. It offers a promise. Something reliable.'[20] More information on branding was given in Chapter 8, in case you missed it.

Some of Peters' thoughts on the comparison of the 'Brand You' world with the 'Employee' world are listed in Table 12.1.

Table 12.1   'Brand you' vs. 'Employee' world

'Brand you' world	Employee' world
Committed to my craft. Intend to be incredibly good at s-o-m-e-t-h-i-n-g	Working assiduously on in-box contents
Willing to take a 'lowly' task if I can turn it into something 'cool'	Don't' try to push bullshit off on me, bro
L-i-v-e for my clients!	I do my job
Am (frequently) angry at our slowness to change	C'est la vie
It's better to ask forgiveness after the fact than permission before (Always!)	Don't expose your butt

Source: Tom Peters (1999) *The Brand You 50: Fifty Ways to Transform Yourself from an Employee into a Brand that Shouts Distinction, Commitment, and Passion*. New York: Alfred A. Knopf, p. 47.

Part of Peters' passion for branding yourself comes from his belief that 90+ percent of white collar jobs will be reinvented and or reconceived in the next decade, and it's up to us to be proactive in order to remain employed. He suggests creating a 'brand equity evaluation' – some of the elements are listed in Exercise 12.4. Exercise 12.5 takes this one step further – developing your brand equity evaluation into an advertisement.

Exercise 12.4 Personal brand equity evaluation

Fill in the boxes below.

Element	Your 2—5 item answers
I am known for …	
By this time next year, I will be known for …	
New stuff I've learned in the last 90 days includes …	
Important new additions in my Rolodex include …	

Exercise 12.5 Develop an advertisement for the brand you

Create a brochure, Yellow Pages advertisement, or web page for the brand you. Pretend people are shopping for the skills you have. What do you have that no one else is offering?

Package yourself

Peters is also a huge fan of packaging. He discusses the importance of exceptional product packaging in several of his other texts, and also discusses how important the 'brand you' package is. One of the issues he discusses is that we tend to hide our personalities at work:

> **Many/most of us suppress our personalities between nine to five.** We are afraid to show just how quirky we really are. So we snuff out our spontaneity and eccentricities ... and nurture Dilbert-esque resentments toward the boss and or our coworkers ... that manifest themselves as passive aggression. Like doing a half-ass job. Guess who gets hurt the most? (Hint: It ain't the boss.)[21]

Peters uses Southwest Airlines to illustrate an organization that does not suppress the personalities of their employees. But how does this relate to packaging? Peters states that packaging is expressed personality: 'For Ford. And Fidelity. For Harvard. And Brown. And McDonald's. And for me. And ... for you.'[22] Peters recommends going to the grocery store or mall and studying great packaging. Look at what makes particular packages stand out. He also recommends reading two books: Thomas Hine's *The Total Package*[23] and Dale Carnegie's *How to Win Friends and Influence People*.[24] Then talk to two or three successful solo practitioners – e.g. graphic artists, lawyers, dentists – and observe how they package themselves.

Exercise 12.6   **Your packaging**

Talk to successful solo practitioners as described above. Then describe how you can use this information to improve your 'packaging.'

Notes

1. Marcus Buckingham and Donald Clifton (2001) *Now Discover Your Strengths*. New York: Free Press.
2. Seth Godin (2003) *Purple Cow*. New York: Portfolio, p. 110.
3. Ibid.
4. Seth Godin (2005) *Free Prize Inside*. New York: Portfolio, p. 39.
5. Ibid., p. 55.
6. Stephen Lundin, Harry Paul, and John Christensen (2000) *Fish! A Remarkable Way to Boost Morale and Improve Results*. New York: Hyperion.
7. Ibid., p. 78.
8. Tom Peters (1999) *Circle of Innovation*. New York: Vintage Books, p. 134.
9. Lundin et al., *Fish!*
10. Isiah Berlin (1993) *The Hedgehog and the Fox*. Chicago: Elephant Paperbacks.
11. Jim Collins (2001) *Good to Great: Why Some Companies Make the Leap ... and Others Don't*. New York: HarperCollins.
12. Ibid., p. 96.
13. Mark Sanborn (2004) *The Fred Factor: How Passion in Your Work and Life Can Turn the Ordinary into the Extraordinary*. New York: Currency Books.
14. Ibid., p. 9.
15. Ibid., p. 11.
16. Ibid., p. 12.
17. Ibid., p. 13.
18. Tom Peters (1999) *The Brand You 50: Fifty Ways to Transform Yourself from an Employee into a Brand that*

Shouts Distinction, Commitment, and Passion. New York: Alfred A. Knopf, p. 5.

19. Ibid.
20. Ibid., p. 6
21. Ibid.
22. Ibid.
23. Thomas Hine (1977) *The Total Package: The Secret History and Hidden Meanings of Boxes, Bottles, Cans, and Other Persuasive Containers.* Boston: Back Bay Books.
24. Dale Carnegie (1998) *How to Win Friends and Influence People.* New York: Simon & Schuster.

Conclusion

A Simmons Professor Emeritus, A.J. Anderson, wrote a book entitled *Problems in Library Management*.[1] I have used several of the cases from his text in my classes, as well as a few of his 'How Do You Manage' cases published in *Library Journal*.[2]

Although the book was published in 1981, many of the issues presented in the cases are real problems faced by libraries today, and many of the issues can be attributed to a lack of marketing – educating politicians, patrons (and non-patrons) about what the library actually does. Unfortunately, there are a lot of people that don't know how valuable the library actually is. It is of critical importance that libraries take a proactive stance to avoid these problems.

On the ALA website there are the all too frequent reports of library closings due to budget cuts, staff layoffs, and the like. I can't help but think that many of them could have been avoided if at the library they had had better marketing.

In the first chapter we discussed problems and barriers to library marketing. Many of these challenges can be overcome though ongoing professional development focusing on developing marketing skills and creating a marketing plan for the library. In many of the other chapters, ways to make the library more innovative were discussed. Some of these ideas may work for your library, many will not. Realizing the need for change is a step in the right direction, particularly if your library is not doing anything to market itself right now. The exercises in each of the chapters will hopefully get the wheels turning and plant the seeds of your marketing plan. I hope you have fun with them and are able to implement these changes in your library.

Notes

1. A.J. Anderson (1981) *Problems in Library Management.* Westport, CT: Libraries Unlimited.
2. Professor Anderson contributed a monthly column to the *Library Journal* for 15 years or so.

Epilogue

Right after I wrote my first book, I vowed never, ever, to write another book again ... and I'm sure some of the people who read the book would have been happy to never hear from me again. Somehow I forgot that vow when I decided to write this book – I gave myself plenty of time and a 1 August 2007 deadline. As July 2007 approached, I cursed myself as I hovered over my laptop during the long, warm, sunny days in my cottage in York, Maine. Never again!! But even as I'm writing this, the seed of another book is taking root – a book that is similar to Seth Godin's *The Big Moo*[1] and *99 Cows*,[2] but profiling remarkable libraries, ones that stand out in the field. If you work for one, or know of one of these remarkable libraries, send me a note at *thebigwhoo@juno.com*. If there is enough interest, I will write the book, but I'll be sure to set a deadline in February ...

Notes

1. Seth Godwin (2005) *The Big Moo*. New York: Penguin.
2. Seth Godwin (2003) *99 Cows*. Dobbs Ferry, NY: Do You Zoom.

Free Prizes

Appendix 1
Case study: Marketing academic libraries

Marketing subject librarians at the Brown University Library

The Brown University Library serves three primary audiences, namely undergraduate students, graduate students, and faculty. Library surveys conducted in 1999, 2001, 2003, and 2005 show that while the library is steadily improving the quality of its service, collection, space, and access, there is still great room for improvement if we are to fully meet and eventually exceed the expectations of our users. The problems shared by our target audience are that they (1) are very busy; (2) seek the best resources for their research but often do not know how to uncover them; and (3) are motivated to produce high-quality scholarship.

Brown undergraduates do not have any required courses and design their academic careers based on their individual interests. This open curriculum environment requires that all library activity (orientation, consultation, instruction, promotion of any services) happens without the benefit of what is typical in many academic environments – a required library connection in a core course.

Undergraduates are confident in their ability to evaluate information, yet they are not very confident in their ability to identify scholarly materials on the open Web. There is a disconnection between the skills that undergraduates want to receive from the library, and the skills the library recognizes they need. Both are important to address, but how we communicate the services and resources will be determined by what our users recognize as important to them.

Graduate students are the faculty of tomorrow. Their needs and practices as students will carry through to their professional teaching research. Many of them also have teaching assistant responsibilities in their departments. Brown University has a responsibility to help them be as successful as possible in all of these endeavors. Graduate students have high expectations for the library services, and are the most critical of Brown Library users in regard to the satisfaction with library service overall.

The library supports faculty in two primary areas: research and teaching. The teaching aspects of library support are in direct face-to-face instruction of library resources, recommended resources for courses, and facilitating course reserves (hard copy, PDF, video, and audio). The research activity of faculty is also facilitated by librarians who order requested resources and anticipate faculty needs in support of their research interests.

The library has a service that is uniquely matched to support the challenges faced by the Brown University student and faculty community: subject librarians who are experts in the resources for their discipline areas. Promoting subject librarians supports the library priorities, as outlined by the University Librarian in March 2006, including access to quality resources when and how users want them. One problem Brown University has is the marketing of subject librarians to our primary user communities. Another library priority is to position the library at the center of campus learning, teaching, and research activity. To achieve this goal, the library continues to expand access to scholarly resources and to partner with key beneficiaries of library services.

To date there has been little organized effort to promote subject librarians. Awareness of them is largely the result of an informal mix of word of mouth, website information, and position titles in e-mail signatures. The only organized communication of the subject librarian services has been primarily targeted at faculty, in particular those who teach first-year seminars, in order to encourage faculty to bring their classes to the library for an instruction session. To this end, the promotion is very much an individual process for each 'selling' his or her services to faculty members one by one. Students in these sessions see and hear the subject librarian present to their class, but the scope of what they can provide is often lost in the din of subject-specific databases, library jargon, and an overwhelming amount of information introduced in a single 50-minute session.

Market mix

With the intent to increase the quality of student research and independent research skills, the Brown University Library seeks to increase awareness of subject librarians, a primary service that directly supports this goal and is currently underexposed. The traditional four 'P's for the marketing mix, as discussed in Chapter 2, are product, price, place and promotion – each of which factors in this effort.

Product

Subject librarians are a service provided by the Brown University Library to support the research and teaching activities of the Brown community. They provide guidance and support for the research process and are experts on the resources in the disciplines they cover. Subject librarians also provide significant support for courses, preparing individualized course guides and providing individual research consultations for all students. Course guides are individualized web guides to resources that support the instructor's syllabus and are accessible from the library homepage and can be linked from WebCT.

There are 20 subject librarians with deep knowledge of resources in over 80 disciplines. Many have doctorates in a subject field, i.e. Chemistry, Egyptology, American History and Political Science, and many others hold multiple masters degrees, mostly a combination of an MLS and a subject specialization such as International Relations, Art History, or Classics. Their skills include up-to-date knowledge of newly arrived titles, as well as the ability to quickly customize research support for courses and individuals. These librarians provide classroom introductions to course-related resources and are available for one-on-one consultations.

Valuable as the subject librarians may be in theory in support of the university's instructional mission, most undergraduates and many graduate students are not aware that they exist. Additionally faculty are not aware of many of the available affiliated services, such as customized course pages.

Price

In terms of a cost evaluation, the library has committed significant funding to staff and support subject librarian positions, yet there is low awareness among all students (graduate and undergraduate) that this service exists to support their academic work. Therefore the cost of inaction is significant. In addition to exploiting the financial investment already made, there is value in increased efficiency of student research skills. Saving students' time in finding research materials and pairing them with an expert in the resources of their discipline is a quantitative method we can use to measure value, and the increased likelihood of higher quality work from students is a qualitative measure.

Place

Library services must coexist in both physical and virtual realms. Users want 24/7 access to library services and resources. Users want access to resources when and how they want them – whether it is face to face with a librarian in the library or online through self-service instruction from their home. The services of a subject librarian will most likely be delivered face-to-face in a one-on-one meeting in the library. However, the interaction may also happen virtually through e-mail, phone, or chat. Additionally, the website is the location where students will access course guides prepared by a subject librarian.

Promotion

The promotional strategies for this project center on using tools that will reach all three primary target audiences, and include e-mail, web promotions, print materials, and administration endorsement. This last item carries unique weight in the community. It is the intent of this project to establish promotional elements and then introduce advocacy by the University Librarian to the Dean of the College, the Dean of the Graduate School, and the Dean of the Faculty. Promoting directly to users and to the organizational leaders who influence them will hopefully be effective. The library intends to communicate messages of time savings and an improved research process.

Promotional mix

The promotional mix for the services provided by subject librarians should be a coordinated combination of the following core components: advertising, personal selling, sales promotion, public relations, and direct marketing. The following breakdown is a recommendation for a promotional mix for the services of subject librarians at the Brown University Library.

Advertising

Advertising will consist of broadcast promotion through posters to be displayed in academic departmental offices and promotional video slides which are displayed in public spaces on campus such as the dining halls and student common areas. The library's website is also a platform for advertising, as is the use of bookmarks with supporting messages printed on them. Some universities, such as the University of Illinois at Urbana-Champaign, have found success in placing advertising limited to their school population of Facebook users.

Personal selling

Personal selling is already a regular practice for many of the Subject Librarians, who rely on their personal interactions with faculty and students to build their business. Sales promotions such as the use of a roving campus reference cart staffed by a subject librarian or prizes for students who schedule a follow-up consultation after attending a library instruction session are suggestions for future implementation. There is a subject librarian who holds office hours in the lobby of a campus building. Her 'Librarian in the Lobby' effort has been highly successful, but has not yet been successfully adopted by others.

Public relations

The public relations efforts associated with the subject librarians which plant positive news stories will likely emerge in a handful of outlets. The library's website has a news section where this service could be promoted. The Sheridan Center for Teaching and Learning publishes a biannual newsletter that is sent to all faculty and graduate students. In September 2006, there was a small article published on the benefits of the course guides produced by subject librarians. There was little response associated with the article, but it is a reliable outlet that can be tapped for future public relations efforts. Other outlets are the campus newspaper, *The Brown Daily Herald*, and the online news site, *The Brown Daily Jolt*.

Sales promotion

The most regularly used promotional avenue taken currently is direct marketing, primarily through the campus e-mail system. The system allows for the targeted selection of students by year and concentration, faculty, staff, and a number of other variations, including an e-mail to all members of the community. How the Brown University Library can best use this system should be explored to ensure that the community does not receive too many similar messages resulting in 'library fatigue.' Another direct marketing tactic is to send flyers or postcards through campus mail.

Planning

In 1999, the Brown University Library went through a strategic planning process. The library is in the early stages now of looking ahead at the next five to ten years to explore strategic directions relevant to the library and university community. At the time of the current strategic plan, the library mission was presented as:

> The Brown University Library, in support of the University's educational and research mission, is the local repository for and the principal gateway to current information and the scholarly record. As such, it is simultaneously collection, connection, and classroom, primarily for the current and future students and faculty of the University, while also serving other colleagues in the University community and our regional, national, and global communities of learning and scholarship. (Brown University Library Strategic Plan, 1999)

In the short-term plan, the library has assessed that initial work should be done to improve awareness across all target users of subject librarians. This plan recommends that a campaign be launched in August 2007 that formalizes the promotional mix stated herein. The ongoing focus on building relationships between subject librarians and faculty will take time, and will continue for the foreseeable future. The library's instruction program must be strengthened in order to improve the perceived value of the service, which will hopefully result in increased confidence of the university community, including our primary users and campus partners, in the valuable role Subject Librarians have in the production of high-quality scholarship.

Links

At the time of the strategic plan, a task force on the educational role of the library made the following recommendations:

1. Develop an effective and aggressive public relations campaign with an emphasis on reaching the under-graduate and graduate student population.

2. Increase student awareness that librarians who are subject specialists and educational consultants are available to help them.

3. Target key student groups such as freshmen, honors and graduate students, and resident counselors for library outreach and public relations efforts.

Eight years later, there have been efforts made to formalize these plans, but they have largely been ad hoc attempts to achieve only portions of these recommendations as they relate to individual projects. A focused marketing effort for subject librarians will likely result in successful execution of these recommendations, and carry over positive impact for overall user perceptions of quality of service relating to the mission statement defined in 1999.

Funding

The library has no single marketing budget. Instead, marketing is handled by individual departments and on a per project basis. The reference department has $3,000 allocated for the biannual pizza event held during exam week. This amount also covers food to printing costs. There are also funds provided to the Scholarly Resources department that can be allocated for outreach and marketing, although those funds are not explicitly set aside. The University Library Administration office has an endowment of $12,000 for publications and an additional $10,000 to fund Friends of the Library promotions, events, and activities. Indirect funding is provided through salaried staff expertise that is applied to marketing effort. The library has staff with design and technology expertise as well as the content and community knowledge necessary for successful marketing. These funding specifications do not include wages.

Staffing

The Brown University Library has no dedicated individual responsible for all marketing activities. The library does recognize the importance of such activity, and the University Librarian has appointed a Library Instruction and Outreach Group made up of six staff members who represent relevant departments. The group consists of two members of the Scholarly Resources department which includes subject librarians, three members from the Reference department, and the Associate University Librarian for Access Services.

An External Relations Officer manages communication with donors, administration, and the Friends of the Library program. Her role is to manage a portion of library communications, and her perspective is important in the execution of library marketing as a whole. The library does have a digital images specialist, available to produce promotional materials, and an Instruction and Outreach Librarian who is skilled at visual communication and has an understanding of the user environment we serve. The adept Web Services Department is able to handle myriad electronic communications. Campus resources that are available for marketing efforts include the highly effective Morning Mail e-mail system and on-campus graphic services for printing.

Research

Traditionally the library has developed services to address a problem or need recognized by the library, such as teaching a new resource or tool, or by the university administration, such as plagiarism. The risks of making decisions in isolation from the target market is that users may not be interested in the product at all or at least not interested in how it is pitched to them. This culture at the Brown Library is shifting towards a user-centric model. User data and feedback will be collected in multiple ways: focus groups, surveys, quantitative data on research consultations with subject librarians, and ongoing discussions with the target audiences.

The Brown student community for the Fall 2006 semester consisted of 6,010 undergraduates, 1,756 graduate students, and 359 medical students. The faculty at the same time was 658, and growing. The library serves these users in the manner outlined, but also is available to support the nearly 3,000 staff members who collectively make the university function day to day.

The library is able to draw on a regular cycle of data upon which to base an understanding of our target market. In the spring of 2005, the library conducted the LibQual+ survey which reported on faculty and student expectations and perceptions of service. Beginning in the summer of 2006, the library has asked users to participate in focus groups, usability tests, and surveys. Surveys have been conducted for incoming students before they come to campus, when they are on campus at orientation, and at the end of library instruction sessions.

A website redesign process also began in the summer of 2006 and included one-on-one usability testing and small focus group conversations about physical and virtual use of library services and resources. The focus groups include undergraduates, graduates, and faculty. These activities are ongoing and provide insights into what users want from the library, how we can connect what we offer with what they do, and how to adapt to their needs. The data collected in the usability testing sessions included user feedback on library services as well as website specific data.

Advocacy

There are a number of on-campus partnerships that the library should continue to build in order to improve awareness of our services among related organizations but also to leverage their relationships with opinion leaders on campus. The primary partnerships which should be fostered are with the Sheridan Center for Teaching and Learning, which works with faculty and graduate students to improve the quality of teaching at the university. Another related group is Teaching and Learning Services in the IT department, which oversees the Instructional Technology Group and the Student Technology Associates program. The Writing Center is an organization that directly reports to the Dean of the College and is housed in the primary campus library building.

Another collection of groups to cultivate as advocates for library services, and Subject Librarians in particular, are the Undergraduate Council of Students, the Graduate Student Council, and departmental staff administrators. This latter group are the gatekeepers to departmental meeting agendas and the departmental knowledge of the 'whos' and 'whats' of the group.

Branding/buzz

While there have not been systematic attempts to create buzz and to formally brand the library, there is interest in doing so. Branding is experience, and care must be taken to ensure all experiences are memorable and positive. The library is launching a six-month training and performance focus on customer service for all front-line library staff, with the hope that improved customer service will result in improved experiences with the library.

Branding is built upon common user experiences, some of which at the Brown University Library are very positive in some cases and in other cases are not. To this end, the library's Reference Services Task Force is conducting a qualitative reference and customer service survey (22–25 April 2007) and the subject librarians are logging all student interactions over a two-week period in April 2007. This data will provide a snapshot into user experiences and desires for service.

Word of mouth has been an effective tool among those Subject Librarians who actively promote it. They use their personal relationships to build positive experiences among faculty and graduate students. Buzz is an interesting area to explore for potential positive impact at the Brown University Library. The library would benefit from transforming 'library fans' who are also opinion leaders in their communities into 'buzz agents.' If the opinion leaders can be identified within our target audiences, who are also library users, we can formalize a two-way communication stream where they communicate how the library is doing and how users perceive our services, and then those messages can be disseminated to the intended audience.

Target marketing

The library has made attempts at marketing to the primary user groups: undergraduates, graduates, and faculty. In the past year, the library has made significant improvements in market research targeting these groups. Some marketing activity has actively employed this newly minted knowledge, and the library is now positioned to move forward with more uniform marketing efforts to target our primary audiences. Subject librarians provide a service that supports all users, but primarily support faculty, graduate students, and third- and fourth-year undergraduates. First- and second-year undergraduates have not declared concentrations and are generally not required to conduct significant original research. Graduate students in particular are a critical audience to target because they not only perform their own research, but many are also teaching assistants who are working with undergraduates.

Conclusions

The complexity of finding and assessing information is increasing, yet the tools that users interface with have not adapted to simplify this process. While this is changing with the advent of user-centric, faceted searching, and next-generation OPAC tools such as WorldCat Local, the disconnect between Brown University users' expectations and practices and the tools that are provided for them are challenging the college to consider its relevance for our users, both real and perceived.

The challenge for this project is to successfully promote and market the services of subject librarians to undergraduate students, graduate students, and faculty. The library has not effectively marketed them as is revealed in the uniform lack of awareness of subject librarians noted in focus groups and usability testing. The marketing efforts that have been successful for graduate students and faculty can largely be tied to effective personal selling on the part of the individual subject librarian. Therefore those individuals without the skills or personalities to take on that role appear not to be as successful. A coordinated marketing effort would spread the marketing activity across numerous channels, and hopefully result in an overall improvement in both user expectations as well as the number of consultations held by subject librarians.

The recommended objectives for this project are to increase the number of students who utilize the research support and consultation services of the subject librarians by 25 percent. In service to faculty, a target goal is to increase the number of classes taught for faculty by 25 percent and to increase the development of high-quality course pages by 10 percent.

Appendix 2
Case study:
Marketing a public library

Waltham Public Library

The Waltham Public Library is located in downtown Waltham, Massachusetts. The town is located nine miles west of Boston. Made up of 59,226 people, the town's population is a diverse collection of races as well as of incomes. In addition, Waltham contains the second largest office market in Massachusetts, behind Boston. The town also contains several parks and historic sites.[1]

Problems

Waltham's diversified population and thriving community profile should make it easy for its library to market to a variety of different groups. However, this library, like many other public libraries, fails to take full advantage of its community when marketing itself. Public libraries have historically not had to think about marketing, and there is still reluctance in the field to do so. Some librarians think that by marketing, they are changing the library's traditional image as a public service into a type of commercial business. However, in order to bring people into the library, the library has to let its patrons know who it is and what it can do for them.

This is not to say that the Waltham Public Library is not attempting to market. The staff are aware that it should be marketed, and different strategies have been attempted. However, marketing is not a top priority in the library. Since Waltham is a thriving community, its library has a huge number of ventures that it could embark on to give itself a greater presence in the community. For instance, as stated before, Waltham has a huge business market. Some of these businesses are large and likely already have their own libraries or research staff. However, most likely there are some smaller companies that might be in need of research assistance. The library could market itself in local business publications or through the Chamber of Commerce to carve out a new niche for itself. Another possibility lies in Waltham's large number of parks and historic sites. The library could partner with these sites to offer events and information about these places. In addition, because Waltham's downtown area has recently undergone a dramatic renovation, the library could put on events pertaining to this historic area. For instance, the library could offer a walking tour of downtown with information on the historic buildings. Many people like to know the local history of their town. While the library provides and promotes many events, such as book talks, it is not taking advantage of all the local resources and opportunities in order to provide a unique and local experience to its patrons. Not all of these opportunities are necessarily feasible, but they represent the wealth of opportunities that the Waltham Public Library has in the community and is not taking.

Marketing mix

The marketing mix involves examining four different aspects to see how they work together in order to conduct more useful and successful marketing initiatives. These aspects, called the four 'P's, were discussed in Chapter 1. Although the Waltham Public Library is on the right track, it has yet to use these four aspects to really enhance its marketing.

Product

The library's products are the services that it provides. This includes the physical collection housed in the library, which includes 155,000 books, over 400 magazines and newspapers, 20,000 CDs, and more than 16,000 videos and DVDs (Waltham Public Library). In addition to the physical collection, the library has subscriptions to numerous databases. The library also belongs to the Minuteman Library Network, which gives its patrons access to other library collections within the network.

The library's products also include other services that it provides, such as staff assistance, special programs, and exhibits. For instance, a service that is always provided is reference assistance. Also, the library has seasonal services. One example of this is in the month leading up to the tax deadline, patrons can go to the library if they have any questions about filing.

Price

Although library services are free to patrons, they still cost money. In this case, the price comes not from how much consumers pay for products, but from how much it costs to supply the products to consumers. This money comes from a budget allotted by the city, tax dollars, donations, and fundraisers. Costs can be direct or indirect. For example, a direct cost comes from a single activity, such as buying library materials and equipment as well as supplying staff and materials for a single event. Indirect costs come from ongoing activities, such as employing permanent staff. Many different costs come into play at the library.

Place

According to Darlene Weingand, the place '... of the marketing mix consists of the channels that link products to consumers.'[2] The most obvious place in the library is the physical building. However, other places exist as well. For instance, the library's website is a virtual place that is growing in popularity for patrons. Instead of going to the physical library, more patrons are choosing to go to the virtual library. The website has become a lucrative place to reach patrons.

Promotion

By considering product, price, and place, the library can decide how and where to promote its products to its patrons. Promotion can be done through a number of avenues, but looking at the previously stated aspects should help to make clear what type of promotion should be used and where.

Although the Waltham Public Library has a grasp of what its products are, how much these products cost, and where it reaches its patrons, it has not used this information to adequately promote its products. In other words, its promotional attempts do not always match its product, place, and price. One place where this is glaringly true is on its website. According to the site, last year it received 996,335 visits.[3] However, the site does not promote the library well. It should have web pages devoted to its programs. Instead, its only venue for promoting events is a very small events calendar. It could also feature new materials to highlight its collection in order to draw patrons into the library. While the site is not terrible, it does not adequately promote the library or its services.

Planning

The Waltham Public Library has the following as its mission statement:

> The Waltham Public Library mission is to provide the city's multi-ethnic, economically diverse population with the print, non-print, electronic, and human resources necessary to meet patrons' primary informational, recreational, and educational library needs.[4]

Goals

1. Develop and maintain outstanding book and audiovisual collections while insuring there are always sufficient circulating copies of popular materials and sufficient subject coverage of high-demand topics.

2. Expand patron and staff access to information through new automation technologies including the Internet, CD-ROMs, and online databases.

3. Expand training and continuing education programs for staff and patrons with special emphasis on new library automation technologies.

4. Expand outreach efforts to guarantee that all city residents, regardless of age, income, education, race, or ethnic origin, feel welcome at the library and know about and have easy access to the variety of programs, services, and resources available to them.

5. Expand cooperative planning at the city (e.g. WALNET), regional (e.g. Minuteman Library Network), and state-wide levels (e.g. Massachusetts Board of Library Commissioners) to improve cost-effective resource sharing (website).[5]

The mission statement affects how the library plans its spending for the year on the collection, equipment, staff training, and outreach. By stating these as its goals, the library puts these issues at the top of the list for what it wants to accomplish.

Links

The mission also affects how the library views its marketing. The fact that the mission statement mentions marketing in its fourth goal (to make sure that all patrons are aware of services, programs, and resources that are available to them) is a huge step in making marketing a major focus. However, according to the library's assistant director, Kate Tranquada, the library has struggled with leaner staff and budget over the past few years.[6] Because of this, marketing, outreach, and public relations have suffered. While this mission statement proves that the library is aware that it needs to strengthen its marketing initiative, it has yet to really take its marketing to the next level.

Funding

The library did not want to reveal its marketing budget. However, the library's marketing budget does not cover much of the marketing for library programs because many of these library programs are sponsored by the Friends group. That being said, the Friends create, print, and fund most of the marketing materials associated with the programs. Since the Friends pay for so much of the marketing, the library should be able to really focus on the few marketing products that it creates and to ensure they are of high quality.

Staffing

No single staff member is responsible for all of the marketing. The director, assistant director, and children's librarian are the staff members most active in marketing, depending on what is being marketed. For instance, the children's program marketing will be done mostly by the children's librarian. In addition, the Friends group does marketing for programs that it creates. The library should really have one person who oversees the marketing so that it has a uniform appearance. This person could also act as a liaison between the Friends and the library in order to make sure that both organizations' marketing materials are consistent.

Research

The library implements research tools such as circulation statistics, surveys, and government demographic data for planning purposes. However, most of this data is used for making decisions about the actual collection rather than for marketing. Tranquada says that the library hopes to use this data for marketing eventually, but it has not done so up to now.[7]

Advocacy

The Friends of the Waltham Public Library has 850 active members. They lobbied to get funds to expand the library and succeeded. In addition, they regularly fight the city to get a decent library budget. They also sponsor many events at the library. For instance, in May they have three events planned. This group serves as a great support for the library but could do so much more in terms of marketing.

Its marketing, like its pamphlets and handouts, should tie in more consistently with the library. For instance, the Friends group has its own logo. While it is great that the group is branding itself, it would be beneficial if its brand tied in more with the library's brand. If, for instance, it included the library's logo somewhere on its handouts, it would strengthen its alliance with the library.

Branding/buzz

The library is trying to brand itself. Many of its fliers contain the same logo that is also on the library's website. The logo also appears on library stationary and business cards. This seems to be the library's attempt to brand itself, which is admirable. However, the branding is not consistent because the logo does not appear on all the fliers. And even on some of the fliers and handouts that it does appear on, it is not prominent. For instance, on the pamphlet that is available at the library's entrance that gives facts and information about the library, the reader does not see this logo until he or she opens up the pamphlet. Instead, it should appear on the cover of the pamphlet so that it is consistent with other handouts.

Another inconsistency arises from the Friends group fliers. The Friends of the Waltham Public Library has its own logo that appears on all of its handouts. This almost makes it seem as though the Friends are completely separate from the library. Even though these handouts are created by the Friends group, they are promoting the Waltham Public Library and should therefore be branded in the same way as other library handouts.

One place where the library is trying to further its brand is on its website. The top of every page of the website contains the library's logo. The website uses maroon and black throughout, creating a consistency. These colors are also found on some of the pamphlets for the library. However, the website has some problems. First of all, it is not up to date. The page that contains the library's hours says that the library is open all Saturdays and Sundays in 2006 with a few exceptions. Since 2006 has passed, patrons probably are not interested in this information. When an organization bills itself as having pertinent and timely information and resources, it should make sure that its information is up to date. In addition to this problem, the website does not contain the library's mission statement. For a library, the mission statement reveals its brand. To not have that available for patrons to see is a mistake.

As for creating buzz, the library says that it has not done enough. The one area that the library can point to where it has begun to create some buzz is through the word-of-mouth success its Spanish-speaking staff member has had in bringing Spanish-speaking patrons into the library.

Target marketing

The library has tried to market itself to specific segments of the population. For instance, it has tried to provide outreach to new immigrants. It has created a guide called 'Services to Immigrants' that is presently being translated into Spanish. This guide lists contacts for newly emigrated Waltham residents. In addition, the library holds ESL classes weekly to try to get this population into the library. It has also tried to build the collection of foreign language works. It has increased the amount of materials in Russian, Chinese, Spanish, Portuguese, and French.

Also, the library's children's department does outreach to both children and families. It also delivers items to daycare providers and works with the local schools. The Young Adults librarian also tries to promote the YA collection through a book club with school librarians at the local high school and middle school.

Conclusions

One easy first step that the library could take is working with the Friends group. Since the Friends group runs most of the library programs, and since it creates all of the marketing for those programs, it needs to make sure that its marketing vision is the same as that of the library. This could be as easy as integrating the library's logo onto its marketing tools and featuring its logo less prominently. This way, instead of appearing to be two completely different organizations, the two will be connected and have a similar brand appearance.

The library should also have one or two designated staff members overseeing the marketing. By doing this, one or two people will be in charge of all marketing and the messages will become more consistent. These staff members could also work with the Friends group to ensure that the messages from both organizations are consistent.

The library should also use the research tools that it already successfully employs to build its collection to learn who it should be marketing to and how it should be doing it. For instance, if it looks at circulation statistics and sees that it has a huge ESL patron population, it needs to continue to cater to this population. The library could also use this information to see what population segments it does not reach. If, for example, through the circulation statistics, the library learns that almost none of the elderly population uses the library, it needs to figure out how it can better market to that population. Since the library most likely does not have a very plentiful marketing budget, it could use this research to figure out how it can more intelligently market. After it performs this research, it could even meet with the Friends group to decide what kinds of other programs can be created to reach these groups.

The Waltham Public Library is on the right track with its marketing. The heads of the library recognize that it is important and should be a priority. Marketing is mentioned in its mission statement. The library is trying to build a brand. All of these are steps in the right direction. Now the library just needs to bring all of these ideas together in order to market to its full potential.

Notes

1. Massachusetts Department of Housing and Community Development (2007) *Waltham – Community Profile*, 20 April; see: *http://www.mass.gov/dhcd/iprofile/315.pdf* (accessed 31 July 2007).
2. Darlene Weingand (1999) *Marketing/Planning Library and Information Services*. Englewood, CO: Libraries Unlimited.
3. Waltham Public Library, 23 April 2007; see: *http://www.waltham.lib.ma.us/index.php*.
4. Kate Tranquada, personal interview, 23 April 2007.
5. Ibid.
6. Ibid.
7. Ibid.

Appendix 3
Selected sample
exercise answers

Exercise 2.1 Creating a marketing mix

A radically new design for a toothbrush:

Huge Savings on Our New Deluxe Toothbrush, *Yuppy Brush*

Buy now for only $10. You will save $20 off the regular price of $30. This Yuppy Brush is an anti-cavity, whitening, cleansing, fresh-tasting toothbrush. In addition, this tooth brush has built-in toothpaste. No more toothpaste to purchase. In fact, no more sweets! This toothbrush has a built-in sweet-tooth satisfier. Yes, this Yuppy Brush will satisfy even the most voracious appetite for sweets. We have them in all sizes, shapes, and colors. Please don't hesitate to try out our new Yuppy Brush. We will give you $10 off your next purchase just for giving this Yuppy Brush a try. You can visit us online any time day or night at *http://www.yuppybrush.com* or visit your local pharmacy or CVS store.

A new wonder drug:

MARIE'S MIRACLE SET

Today, we are proud to announce our new Miracle Set. You can live the dream life you have always wanted. With Miracle Set, you can have a more rich and rewarding life. Just rub this cream on your face each morning and night and watch those wrinkles totally disappear before your eyes. No need to purchase those expensive jars of creams, moisturizers, and lotions. Save your money and purchase Miracle Set, a four-in-one combination that cleanses, tones, moisturizes, and enhances your natural skin tones. You too can have your dreams come true for a more beautiful face by purchasing Marie's Miracle Set for only $5, plus shipping and handling. We know you will not want to be without this wonder drug. In fact, we have a limited time offer of two sets for only $8. Buy now while supplies last, or visit our website at *http://www.miracleset.com*.

Library program: 'Reading to Infants':

Please visit the Blake Memorial Library's 'Reading to Infants' program on Thursday mornings at 9:30. Abby Smith will be reading the story and talking to caregivers about the tools for your infant to become a more successful reader later on in life. By reading daily with your infant, you will be helping to enhance their pleasure in reading, developing their reading comprehension, and creating a bond with your child that will last forever. Light refreshments will be served. Please call the library at 802/439-5338 for further information.

Exercise 2.3 Connecting marketing to mission

Target service: Interlibrary loan (ILL).

The library mission: The mission of the college addresses the lifelong learning needs of a diverse community, including (among other things) developmental skills, career preparation and industry involvement, and transfer education for those planning to move on to four-year institutions and beyond.

How the target service contributes to the mission: It allows all members of the campus community (students, staff, and faculty) access to a huge array of materials, free of charge. The library is, by necessity, limited to holdings that directly support a community college curriculum, but ILL allows the library to further support the mission. For example, developmental students can request high-school texts and works aimed at the lower-level reader. Transfer students can access detailed research materials and graduate-level items. Students doing vocational and career research can request training manuals or test preparation guides that aren't freely available online.

Also:

Annual Event

Join the *Blake Memorial Library's First Annual Garden Tour* for only $15 (registered borrowers and seniors, $10; under 6 free).

Stroll through the gardens in your community and witness some unbeatable arrangements. Take advantage of those incomparable blooms made doubly enchanting by their irresistible fragrance. Notice how vigorous, well-branched bushes and trees make a magnificent focal point in the landscape. Learn through the experts what plants survive the harsh Vermont winter weather. Learn how to cope with that rock-filled soil by building a stone wall and experiencing that 'granite kiss.' Most importantly, as Mr Rogers used to say, 'Meet the people in your neighborhood!'

End your tour at the *Blake Memorial Library* for freshly squeezed lemonade and homemade treats. Borrow one of our new garden-inspired books, or let us explain the online sources for some of the world's finest garden products that guarantee complete satisfaction with every plant you purchase.

Exercise 2.4 Promotion

Press kit

Professional looking pocket folder with a window identifying the name of the library. In the folder, include CVs of library employees; include a compilation of all positive press releases; include letters of support from the movers and shakers in your community; include sample library budget with specific information about collection development, operating costs, and future project plans. Also include a small promotional item, such as a paperclip or magnet, that will help the item make it to the reporter's desk. Guidebook (PDF).

Photographs — Submit a digital photo to your local newspapers each time you have a library program or event. Make certain the photo includes people (especially children), such as photos of a caregiver reading to a child, or library staff helping a senior on the computer, or a student doing homework, etc.

New releases — Have a column in your local paper entitled *Local Library News*. Submit an article discussing what is happening and answer the questions to who, what, when, and why.

News memo for quick release — Call your local radio station and ask them to make an announcement about your library's event as time warrants.

Column item — E-mail your events for the next couple of months to your local newspapers with the dates all in caps and ask them to make certain your events are given publicity.

Feature story — Submit digital photos to your local newspapers along with a story about the event. Have someone in your community take the photos and give

	them credit under the photos. Make certain the photos include people in your community.
News conference	Emphasize the positive and avoid the negative. Give effusive praise especially to the movers and shakers in your community for affording you the opportunity to talk about the library. Give out your 'business' card.
Special event	Call radio station; e-mail your patrons (blind carbon copy to avoid unsolicited e-mails); make certain the event has been published in the local newspapers; put flyers on local bulletin boards; put your event on a sidewalk sign.
Collateral materials (i.e. bumper stickers, bookmarks, buttons)	Make bookmarks with an illustration of your library's building with the library's address, hours, story time, telephone and fax numbers, e-mail address, and website. Bumper sticker: *FREA*DOM @ BLAKE MEMORIAL LIBRARY; same for sticker and button with a logo.
Annual report	Brag about your local programs, circulation numbers, library visits,
Posters	Download an image from the Internet (via Google) and put on flyers using Microsoft Publisher.

Brochures	Again download an image from the Internet (Google) and put on flyers using Microsoft Publisher.
Direct mail	Have a sign-up sheet at your circulation desk for patrons to submit their e-mails. When an event is happening in your library, e-mail EVERYBODY, blind carbon copy (bcc) only.
Public service announcements	Call the radio station and ask them to announce your event as time allows. They usually will take announcements at the last minute.
Newsletters	Have everyone in their respective departments tell you what they are accomplishing and put it in a newsletter. Again emphasize the positive. Also list the names of the volunteers and how they are helping the library. Always put the names of the people who are helping with the library functions.
Speeches/public appearances	For example, attend a local Rotary Club meeting and talk about the upcoming events at the library, or give a list of the new titles of print and non-print material. Take a couple of titles that would have audience appeal and give the gist of the stories. Disseminate

	handouts with the library's name and hours and URL of the website.
Media presentations	A PowerPoint presentation (you have not used) about your library would be best. Visuals always capture attention and sustain interest.

Exercise 4.1 Trends

Faith Popcorn's 'trends' that can correspond to library services:

- *Small indulgences*. People are willing to pay reasonable, relatively low prices for things they identify as a little bit indulgent. Some university and college libraries offer 'special borrower' cards to the general public, allowing them borrowing privileges. This could be considered a small indulgence to those unaffiliated individuals who seek upper-level or specialized reading material for personal amusement or personal betterment. Alumni borrower cards, as a special category, allow former students to retain an affiliation with their past.

- *Vigilante consumer*. Many libraries offer business and consumer research tools. These are valuable services to the consumer who wants to know more about the companies they buy products from. This includes both the curious consumer ('I want to find an environmentally friendly car manufacturer') and the angry consumer ('I need statistics and other information to support my boycott of this car manufacturer').

- *99 lives*. Most people in our society are overworked and overwhelmed, and their time is precious. Several recent developments have aimed to speed up traditional library services: online book renewal, online reference chat (or e-mail reference), self check-out stations, e-books that can be read from home.

- *Cashing out.* Basically, people want to simplify their lives. What better way than to get rid of all those books cluttering up your home and just borrow them from the library, one by one, as you want or need to read them? Cancel your cable and work your way through the library's feature films *and* educational videos! Get rid of that home computer and those wasteful hours of Internet surfing, and spend an hour or two per week using the library's public computers for any web-based necessities!

- *Ergonomics.* People want services that fit them, specifically. Some library trends along these lines are online catalogs that allow users to set up profiles with wish-lists and so forth (like online bookstores), and catalogs that allow 'social tagging' (the user can attach their own keywords to book records to make future retrieval easier for themselves or like-minded others).

Appendix 4
Sample marketing plan

Introduction

Prince George's County, Maryland is a diverse, growing suburban county located to the east and south of the city of Washington, DC. The county covers 485 square miles. As of 2005, it had a population of 846,123. As of 2005, 226,928 of this population were young people under the age of 18. Clearly, doing outreach to this population will benefit the library and ensure continued usage of, and funding for, the Prince George's County public library system.

The Prince George's County Memorial Library System (PGCMLS) consists of 19 branches. Surratts-Clinton Public Library, where I work, is one of three that service the southern end of the county. The county's designation of this area as a future National Defense and Technology Corridor means plans are afoot for 15,000 units of new housing, 2 million square feet of new retail, and six new schools. It is vital that the library system take action now to prepare for this growth opportunity.

The focus of this project is to explore ways to increase circulation of materials and implement a campaign to encourage customers to sign up for library cards. It will also explore ways to regain lost or stolen materials and to woo back customers who may be reluctant to use the library because of fines accrual and misperceptions about library policy. (For instance, some customers believe that there is a sign-up fee charged for acquiring a library card.)

Section 1 outlines a campaign to increase sign-ups for library cards. Section 2 discusses a book return day. Section 3 covers a fines read-off. Finally, Section 4 outlines a few miscellaneous marketing ideas to be undertaken by library staff.

Section 1: Increase library card sign-up

Intention

Increase library card sign-up among children, teens, and adults. A significant number of teens and adults in Prince George's County do not possess library cards. Many parents check out books for children with their own card and don't sign their children up for juvenile cards. This may be partly attributable to a reluctance to be the responsible party if their children inadvertently lose or damage items, as PG County utilizes a collection agency for unpaid fines and lost items. It may stem from an understandable desire to monitor their child's reading choices to ensure wholesome selections.

Unfortunately, declining to sign up a child for a library card may also occur because the parent has a low level of interest in reading. Reluctant or non-readers often fail to perceive the value of resources offered by the public library. This is detrimental, as teens require a parent to be physically present in the library in order to sign off on a library card application. Lack of parental involvement hampers teens' attempts to perform research for homework assignments, since they can't check out books.

Encouraging customers to sign up for library cards will inform reluctant reader adults of the advantages of a library card; increase the number of items in circulation; empower children and young adults to make responsible choices; reduce the number of paper guest tickets printed for public computer use; and reduce the number of items that 'disappear' because a perpetrator didn't have a library card.

Brainstorm

Come up with a name and slogan for the library card program. Check with ALA or other library organizations to see if similar programs have been implemented. Can we adapt them to Prince George's County? September 2007 is Library Card Sign-Up Month ... a perfect time to launch this campaign!

Household survey

Create a branded survey form to distribute to households within five miles of each branch. Additionally, create an identical survey in Surveymonkey.com and send an invitation to all e-mail addresses currently in the library's customer database.

Questions to ask in the survey include:

1. Age of respondent.

2. Number of people in their household, and their ages.

3. How often do they visit the local public library?

4. What do they use the library for?

5. How many people in the household have a library card?

6. If they do not currently have a library card, why don't they have one? (Use multiple choice responses here, e.g. 'Don't have time to get one,' 'Don't think it's important,' and also leave a choice of 'Other' and two blank spaces for them to write/type a response if they choose to do so.)

7. What can the library do for them, e.g. what kinds of services can it provide to them?

8. Recommendations for programs?

In return for responding to the survey, participants will receive a coupon for $2 off an order at McDonald's, Wendy's, Taco Bell, or Super Chicken. If they physically bring in the survey, library staff will immediately give them a coupon. If they use Surveymonkey.com, they will be able to click to a secure site on the PGCMLS website where they can print out a coupon.

Needed:

■ Research into library card membership drive campaigns in other public libraries/counties.

■ Briefing for all branch managers and staff – share ideas and survey questions; staff suggestions for additional questions to ask in survey.

■ Cost analysis of price for a branded survey (may be possible to create in-house by PR team; survey forms then outsourced to a local printer).

■ Names of local printing companies – would one be willing to donate materials and time (or drop the price) in return for a 'sponsored by ... <fill in name here>' byline at the bottom of the survey?

■ Outreach to local restaurants (McDonald's, Wendy's, Taco Bell, Super Chicken, Papa John's Pizza, or other) to persuade them to participate in the library card survey gift coupon program.

■ An informational brochure, prepared by the public relations staff, to address the ways in which a library card is beneficial, what customers can do with one, whether a cost is involved, and why it's important to report a lost or stolen card to avoid identity theft.

■ Discuss with IT team whether it's possible to link a Surveymonkey.com questionnaire with secure area of library website to provide point-and-click access to coupons.

Offer incentives for teens and/or adults who sign up for library cards

■ Donations from corporate sponsors:

- Pizza from Papa John's Pizza. If an *entire family* comes in to sign up for library cards, they'll get a free Papa John's pizza. The number of toppings offered is equivalent to the number of family members, e.g. 3 people = 3 toppings.
- Coupon from Wal-Mart offering discount on school supplies.
- One free music download or ringtone, courtesy of Verizon Wireless.

■ Prize draw:

- Each customer who signs up for a library card will be entered into a draw for an iPod or mp3 player. There will be one Adult (age 18+) winner, one Teen (age 13–17) winner, and one Child (age 6–12) winner.
- An mp3 prize would be a great tie-in opportunity to promote the library system's audiobook and eBook holdings.

- The 'Child' category will require a device that appeals to children, such as a Leapster Learning System, or some kind of electronic product that appeals to the 6–12 age demographic.

Needed:

- Outreach to local businesses/corporations for prize donations.
- Money for purchase of prizes.

In-house possibilities

In the event that we are not able to acquire sponsorship and support from local commercial entities, the library can offer 'in-house' reward options.

- *Extra computer time.* Library will design a laminated coupon card that gives the user one extra hour of computer time for 10 applications. Card will have space for cardholder's name. Computer time can be used at any point and has no expiration date. However, cardholder *must* check in at the reference desk, since a library staff member will have to make them an extended computer reservation. Staff member will punch a hole in the card each time it is used. Cardholder must show his/her library card in order to utilize extra time option. This will prevent one card from circulating among multiple users. Time on PCs can't be donated to others. Cardholder not permitted to use card for an entire day. Limit is one extra hour per visit.
- *Book swap.* Customers may drop off unused books for a book trade table. Customers can take up to two free books from book sale cart or book trade table in return for signing up for a library card.